BEGIN WHERE YOU ARE

Compiled by

Turner Wyatt

Edited by

Mary Crow, Andrea Gibson, Joseph Hutchison,
Bobby LeFebre, David Mason, and Julia Seldin

Introduction by Khadijah Queen

THE CENTER FOR LITERARY PUBLISHING
Colorado State University
Fort Collins

BEGIN WHERE YOU ARE

The Colorado Poets Laureate Anthology

For information about permission to reproduce selections from this book, write to:
The Center for Literary Publishing
Attn: Permissions
9105 Campus Delivery
Colorado State University
Fort Collins, Colorado 80523-9105.

ISBN: 978-1-885635-98-3 (hardcover)
ISBN: 978-1-885635-97-6 (paperback)
ISBN: 978-1-885635-99-0 (ebook)

Library of Congress Cataloging-in-Publication Data
Names: Crow, Mary author editor | Gibson, Andrea (Poet) author editor | Hutchison, Joseph author editor | LeFebre, Bobby, 1982– author editor | Mason, David, 1954– author editor | Seldin, Julia editor | Wyatt, Turner editor | Queen, Khadijah writer of introduction
Title: Begin where you are : the Colorado poets laureate anthology / edited by Mary Crow, Andrea Gibson, Joseph Hutchison, Bobby LeFebre, David Mason, Julia Seldin, and Turner Wyatt ; introduction by Khadijah Queen.
Description: Fort Collins : The Center for Literary Publishing, Colorado State University, [2025] | Featured poets include Andrea Gibson (laureate 2023–2025), Bobby LeFebre (laureate 2019–2023), Joseph Hutchison (laureate 2014–2019), David Mason (laureate 2010–2014), Mary Crow (laureate 1996–2010), Thomas Hornsby Ferril (laureate 1979–1988), Milford E. Shields (laureate 1954–1975), Margaret Clyde Robertson (laureate 1952–1954), Nellie Burget Miller (laureate 1923–1952), and Alice Polk Hill (laureate 1919–1921).
Identifiers: LCCN 2025040843 (print) | LCCN 2025040844 (ebook) | ISBN 9781885635983 hardcover | ISBN 9781885635976 paperback | ISBN 9781885635990 ebook
Subjects: LCSH: American poetry—Colorado—20th century | American poetry—Colorado—21st century | Poets laureate—Colorado | LCGFT: Poetry
Classification: LCC PS591.P63 B44 2025 (print) | LCC PS591.P63 (ebook)
LC record available at https://lccn.loc.gov/2025040843
LC ebook record available at https://lccn.loc.gov/2025040844

Cover design by Hayley Kirkman
Illustrations by Ethan Duck

To our friend Andrea Gibson

None of this is poetry.
It is just the earth
being who she is . . .

CONTENTS

PREFACE

Turner Wyatt

This is not a book about poets; it's a book about poetry, and the power of place. Most important, it is an attempt to increase access to poetry for all Coloradans.

I'm a social entrepreneur, so I have no business editing a book like this one. Yet the idea for it came to me in 2023, when I was involved in co-creating the Durango Poet Laureate Program. I was doing a lot of thinking about poets laureate, learning as much as possible about this mysterious role that many important writers have filled over the centuries. Who are the laureates, and what do they do? Why do they exist? I bought *The Poets Laureate Anthology*, edited by Elizabeth Hun Schmidt, which gathered poems by every US poet laureate from Joseph Auslander in 1897 through W. S. Merwin in 2010. I naively thought, "Cool! Now

I'll buy the *Colorado Poets Laureate Anthology*." But I quickly discovered that none existed. This puzzled me, so I asked my friend, then–Colorado Poet Laureate Bobby LeFebre, "How does this not exist?"

I knew Bobby from a past life of health equity activism in Denver. I had been working for years to address the fact that lower-income and rural areas and communities of Color tend to have less access to healthy food. Bobby has long known that the same is true in these populations for poetry. What if this book could change that, or at least take a step in the right direction? Bobby introduced me to the just previous poet laureate, Joe Hutchison, who introduced me to Dave Mason, who introduced me to Mary Crow. Months later, a hero of my generation was elected as the newest Colorado poet laureate, Andrea Gibson.

The State of Colorado provides a stipend for the poet laureate (as of recently). But it's tiny, not nearly enough to compensate for the demands of the position, such as presentations, readings, workshops, interviews, introducing poetry to young students, and working with teachers to integrate poetry into their classes. In general, funding for poetry programming is fickle and scarce. Our hope is that this book will foster a new, more sustainable earned-revenue model for poetry funding.

We formed an editorial committee—Andrea Gibson, Bobby LeFebre, Joseph Hutchison, David Mason, Mary Crow, and Julia Seldin—that met regularly for over two years to create this book. We started a nonprofit organization and applied for grants and sought donations to support our idea. We worked as a team. We made consensus decisions, which felt clunky but important. In every meeting, I looked around the room at people from different backgrounds, of different ages, with different poetic styles, all of whom agreed that poetry needed to be more accessible to more people across Colorado.

A portion of the sales from this book will be donated to our nonprofit organization focused on increasing the equity of poetry access in Colorado. Consider your reading of it to be a form of activism or, better yet, a vote of dollars. We will use the funding to do poetry programming in parts of Colorado where the poet laureate has rarely visited because of funding constraints.

Established in 1919, the Colorado Poet Laureateship is the second-oldest state poet laureateship in the US (after California). Why not New York or Massachusetts? David Mason offered an explanation: Unlike the East, where creative expression is ubiquitous, the West couldn't take its arts for granted. I'm honored to have been a part of this project, which I think continues the tradition of prioritizing poetry in Colorado in spite of a rugged, sometimes problematic history.

I hope this book provides a contrast to this past. By asking, in the words of the 1980s Colorado Poet Laureate, Thomas Hornsby Ferril, how far have we come?, we are begged to answer, how far have we yet to go? In our society, in our policies, in our writing, I hope we let the land shape our meaning as it has for the poems in this book. As our title (also Ferril's words) suggests, it's best to begin this work at home.

—TURNER WYATT, MAY 2025

EDIT

August 2025

And then, after working on this book together for two years, in July 2025, months before publication, Andrea Gibson passed away. Our team looked around, grieving with the rest of the world, honored to be among those who had the opportunity to work with someone who has been called the Rumi of our time and "the Queer nation's genius savior poet." It seemed for everyone who knew Andrea, including the millions of strangers who considered them a friend, the world paused.

There was a memorial service at the Mercury Cafe in Denver (as in Andrea's op-ed in *Westword*, "When I Die, Scatter My Ashes at the Mercury Cafe"). Celebrities and poets took the stage to cover Andrea's poems. One asked the audience, "Raise your hand if you ever wanted to leave this world, and Andrea kept you here." There must have been a hundred hands reaching toward the lights strung across the ceiling.

Andrea took on this project when they had already had cancer for two years, when it had already been deemed incurable. While I'm gutted that Andrea didn't live to see this book come to fruition, I'm touched to think that it was a part of the last, magic-making years of their life. I sense there are many of us out there who see Andrea's departure as the perfect, final gift of an angel, here to teach us how to be more presently attuned to life, how to love better, how to make change.

Andrea's participation in this project made us feel like we were doing something special. And we were. Now, we (we all) are humbled to participate in the carrying of their magic toward a new day, and yes, toward home.

BEGIN WHERE YOU ARE

INTRODUCTION

Khadijah Queen

Colorado's landscape is uniquely suited to poetry. During my eight years on the Front Range, I began to write nature poems more than I ever had before. Places like Estes Park, Barr Lake, Chatfield State Park, and Cherry Creek State Park reactivated a childhood love for the natural world that I know won't ever leave me again no matter where I might travel. The majesty of Colorado, and the undeniable connection of its people to that natural beauty—whether they live in larger cities or more rural environments—offer a unique and rich canvas from which to, as Toni Morrison has said, "do language."

That "doing" of language means marrying words with action, creativity with connection. Serving as the poet laureate of any city or state requires a deep commitment to that engagement. To step away from one's solitary work and invent new ways of reaching people takes a sense of play as well as seriousness. Luckily, poems can contain both sensibilities, and as poets use language to invite connection to the full spectrum of human awareness, for subject matter it makes sense to turn to the land and people—from Fruita to Fort Collins, from Leadville to Littleton, from Boulder to Basalt, from Durango to Denver, from Manitou Springs to Colorado Springs—surrounding us. As poets, we wish to tap into as many senses and emotions as we can. We aim to express the inexpressible through what we observe in order to make real-life connections off the page. Colorado offers no shortage of such chances.

Still, the challenge for the poet laureate remains communicating the value of poetry, becoming an ambassador, of sorts, for what the twentieth-century poet, essayist, and journalist Muriel Rukeyser considered to be a resource—poetry as a holding space for contradiction and a vehicle for understanding self and others. Part of the reason poetry can seem mysterious is our reluctance to take time in that holding space. Another reason: a sometimes forced disconnection from how we feel in order to get through our days and lives, especially when it comes to more difficult emotions. Andrea Gibson writes: "We live in a culture that pushes down emotions. Poetry awakens them."

Gibson's poems tell feeling-rich, wide-awake stories with straightforward language that carries the kind of emotional heft that enforcers of silence can only fail to suppress. The intimate and devastating impact of drug addiction appears alongside the grace of sports heroes nearing physical flight, the "I" as strong in its most vulnerable moments because love insists on its own endurance. Experiencing recurring grief and the everyday violence of bias, facing illness and mortality, the speaker in Gibson's poems cries, prays, suffers, fevers, pains—yes—but delights too, proclaims: "I know how to build a survival shelter / from fallen tree branches, packed mud, / and pulled moss," recognizing the earth's materials as vital to healing.

Bobby LeFebre's poems acknowledge lineage through both place and people, documenting the difficult "struggle of land and language and people and politics" and the "beautiful paradox" of faith. Stories of grandparents and Lyft drivers give both warnings and wisdom. Simplicity holds tactile beauty, and ordinary encounters echo multiple histories, "many things existing . . . at the same time." Corn and sun and chiles recur, find bright resonance in hands and on skin, offer sustenance, and help to narrate "a future that vows to never forget its past."

Similarly retaining a deep connection to the wider world, Mary Crow writes of "horizon's eclipse / sliding toward / mountains," keeping readers aware of "the tremendous still / in us" in our state. Her poems stand out as traveling in memory, observing "how small human life looked" next to rarefied monuments, unafraid of admitting fear or loneliness, desire or desperation. Traveling has a way of sharpening observations of the self, and Crow's poems don't shy from the cuts. Even at the most unexpected moments, her poems still seek "a glimpse of the sublime."

Joseph Hutchison is a rooted watcher. His poems document the movement of people, animals, and time. He also notices the smallest of actions in the landscape, such as how "the dreaming grass / flutters in its sleep" without neglecting the ordinary grandeur of "windy canyon shadows / high over kivas and cliff-houses." Too, he notes transformations both without and within, the rewards and costs of those changes: "It's your natural openness / I want to enfold me. But then / you'd become city; or you'd hide / away your wildness to save it."

David Mason's work haunts and breaks taboos, carries us in the language of memory through "mesa country," imagining—craving—a potential connection with "the remnants of a people who moved through, / migrating hunters five millennia past." As laureate, he found connection to audiences large and small, diligently committing to the work of sharing poetry statewide. While realizing that "poets have to confront the fact that much of the world finds their efforts unquantifiable," in his travels all over the state Mason found personal joy as well as "people hungry for the life of poetry." Indeed, the places he visited served as inspiration, and his songlike poems conjure a world where "every mountain rose up to its limit."

"The sky precipitates its hue," writes Milford E. Shields in the poem "San Juan Basin," an ode to an ancient place in the Four Corners. The poem praises how "deepening shades blend swiftly down, / Fuse outer mountains into crown, / Then racing in more vivid sheen / They grow into a sea of green"—using colors as a kind of visual transformation. Serving for over two decades, Shields infused his poems with exuberance and a sense of awe of the natural world, and the divine forces that link living things to one another.

The first Colorado poet laureate, Alice Polk Hill, used her influence and energy to lobby for and create the position over a century ago. Her poems adhere to traditional forms, with exuberant rhymes that praise faith and family without shying away from discussing topics like death and grief, longing and worry. One poem addresses the poet's young daughter, her namesake, lovingly highlighting the child's innocence with a protective layer of parental hope. Hill expresses fervently that young Alice will, under angels' protection, "conquer all foes within, without" in her life.

Hill's successor, Nellie Burget Miller, wrote as one of the "country-folks" in praise of ordinary joys. Enchanted by kittens, bees, hollyhocks, the "scent of fresh-dried linen, and the warm earth / After rain," she "loved homely things" while still observing the larger world. The poems meditate on history, faith, and dreams yet remain grounded in the honest experiences of the everyday present: "Wildest fancies have a grain of truth stuck in the sieve."

Poems by Leadville's own Margaret Clyde Robertson, who served as laureate in the early 1950s, offer us portraits of a population dealing with the unpredictable realities and real dangers of mining life and enliven that moment in the area's history, when "Leadville was mad as Babylon." The poems' dialect and simple rhyme schemes bring to mind camp songs and stories, with balanced doses of humor and warning.

World War I veteran and journalist Thomas Hornsby Ferril, Colorado's poet laureate during the 1980s, also reflects on history and adds a deep sense of the passage of time. Reversals of expectation abound, showing a sharp intellect and an unflinching understanding of reality. His tight lyrics are straightforward and stark, telling us that "War is ever twice as near / As the nearest town." They refuse to hide from difficulty or ugliness, in one poem recalling a child's accidental death. He uses an image of a machine turned deadly in order to show us—not tell us—the larger implications beyond individual tragedy: "Lip of the bulldozer against the skull, / Churning the dead to furrows of new exile." In the current moment, his words resonate, and his curiosity about other humans and their stories reminds us that "beyond the sundown is tomorrow's wisdom." We deserve a present and a future in which, Ferril proclaims, "Love can hold you ever."

I think the earliest laureates would be thrilled with the poets who have served in their stead, in both creative and community endeavors. To perform and to teach are acts of enormous generosity and courage. To share one's personal experiences in poems, spinning those experiences into stories that readers can connect and relate to, is also such an act. The generosity of these poets laureate shines in their deeds as much as their words. And they do so with humility, enthusiasm, and joy.

Bobby LeFebre writes: "The poet manifests, evokes, and makes tangible the visions and love that live within us all." Such manifestation and evolution, I agree, are the work of the poet; to agree to expand that practice publicly, in service to as vast and diverse a state as Colorado, takes a great deal of imagination and fortitude. This anthology represents the tangible openness of the people of our state to receive that work with the same love with which it is offered. It has been my honor to have also called Colorado home, and to have this chance to praise in prose the lush and affirming poetry of these laureates in what I hope will be the first volume of many.

ANDREA GIBSON

Laureate 2023–2025

ONE OF THE MOST CELEBRATED and influential spoken word poets of our time, Andrea Gibson was appointed poet laureate of Colorado in 2023. Best known for their live performances, Gibson changed the landscape of what it means to attend a "poetry show." Gibson's poems center around LGBTQ issues, gender, feminism, mental health, and social justice. The winner of the first Women's World Poetry Slam, Gibson wrote seven award-winning books and seven full-length albums. Their live shows became loving and supportive ecosystems for audiences to feel seen, heard, and held through Gibson's art. Gibson authored six full-length collections of poetry, including *You Better Be Lightning* (Button Poetry, 2021) and *Lord of the Butterflies* (Button Poetry, 2018). Gibson is a two-time winner of the Independent Publisher's Award (in 2022 and 2019), as well as a three-time Goodreads Choice Awards Finalist. In 2017, Penguin Books published *Take Me with You*, an illustrated collection of Gibson's most beloved quotes, and in 2019, Chronicle Books published their first nonfiction endeavor, *How Poetry Can Change Your Heart*.

> The first time I read a poem on a stage I was at an open mic in Boulder, Colorado, in my early twenties. I was so nervous the audience could not hear my voice over the rattling of the paper in my hands. But the next week I bussed to Denver and attended my first poetry slam, and continued to bus down several times a week for years. I never felt so welcomed and at home anywhere.

I studied writing in college, but most of what I know about poetry I learned from the poets of Colorado. They taught me how to trust my voice. How to tell the truth in a way that inspires action. And above all—they taught me that being a poet isn't so much about how we show up to the page but how we show up to the world.

For twenty-five years now my most constant creative desire has been to make this transformative art form accessible to more and more people. Most of us have a favorite song. I love the idea of everyone also having a favorite poem. In workshops, readings, and events I work to share poems that connect communities, engender empathy, and open readers to new perspectives through the sparkle and delight of elevated language. While it is difficult to change a stubborn mind, I've seen poetry of all kinds change people's hearts in an instant.

As I write this I am almost a year into my term as Colorado's tenth poet laureate. I've done countless events in which I've witnessed people of all ages and backgrounds fall in love with poems. We live in a culture that pushes down emotions. Poetry awakens them. The world puts a cubicle around our wonder, and poetry inspires awe. Watching communities throughout the state uncover their own astonishment has been one of the sweetest gifts of my life, and I am so grateful for the treasure of this time.

—ANDREA GIBSON

ACCEPTANCE SPEECH AFTER SETTING THE WORLD RECORD IN GOOSEBUMPS

I wasn't, by any means, a natural.
Was not one of those wow-hounds
born jaw-dropped. I was tough in the husk.
Went years untouched by rain. Took shelter
seriously, even and often especially
in good weather, my tears like teenagers
hiding under the hoods of my eyes,
so committed they were to never falling
for the joke of astonishment.

When I was told there were seven
wonders of the world, I trusted the math,
believed I had seen none of them.
Of course beauty hunted me.
It hunts everyone. But I outran it, hid
in worry, regret, the promise of an afterlife
or a week's end.

Then one day, in a red velvet theater
in New Orleans, I watched Maya Angelou
walk on stage. Seventeen slow steps to the mic.
She took a breath before speaking,
and I could hear god being born in that breath.

My every pore reached out like a hand
pointing to the first unsinkable lotus
in the bayou of the universe.
I'd never felt anything like it.
Searched the encyclopedia
for the feeling's name when I got home:

"Goosebumps."

Afterwards, I thought—*I can do this.*
Started training morning to night,
tore the caution tape off my life
and let everything touch it.

Allen Iverson on the television
in his first season with the Sixers,
crossover sharp as a V of sparrows
flying through the paint like Michelangelo's brush:
272 goosebumps.

My baby sister, sober for the first time
in thirteen years, calling to tell me
she just noticed our mother's eyes are green:
505 goosebumps.

One day, my friend scored tickets
to a Prince concert. Tiny venue.
I was right behind the sound booth.

Prince's entire band that evening—women.
At the end of the show the sound person
turned around and whispered, *He didn't play
one song on his setlist the whole night.*

I live on stages. I know what it is
to scratch a plan, but not the whole trip
and still arrive to your destination
two hundred years before your time:
421 (artist formerly known as) goosebumps.

But that's just the fancy stuff.
Some of them came from simple facts—
It rains diamonds on Jupiter.
Blood donors in Sweden receive a thank you
message when their blood is used.

One night in Michigan, my friend,
still undiagnosed, could not uncurl
her fingers to strum her guitar,
so she sang the chords instead.
It was the first time in my life I'd seen pain
become an instrument:
10 dozen goosebumps
for each and every note plucked up from
the string section of her refusal to silence
her dream.

After that, nothing in the world was gray.
Even the movie of my past was released
in color. The oldest man in my hometown
could not get to the door to listen
to our carols so we went inside and sang
at his bedside instead. Twenty-four boots
on the front step catching snowflakes
with their tongues: 776 goosebumps.

At one point everything started doing it:
A sincere apology, an enemy's love poem.
The moon rising over the continental divide.
My love and I thought it was a car
driving off a cliff, and suddenly
nothing in the world was dying.
You ever felt that? A split second
when nothing in the world is dying?
888 goosebumps, and the next day
I sharpened a tiny ax
so I could split the seconds myself.
Too much lives in a moment
to not feed it to the fire in the heart, slow.

A Missoula treehouse filled with candlelight.
The octopus documentary.
The biggest dog in the shelter
hiding behind a teacup chihuahua,

and the woman who came to adopt a cat
taking all three of them home.

Me, at home, two months into chemotherapy
watching all of my eyelashes fall onto my cheekbones
and realizing that was 400 wishes
I wouldn't have made otherwise.

There is no escaping
the magic now. Beauty caught me
and never let me go.
And the thing about the world record
is—if someone breaks it after me,
and they *will* break it after me,
I will love that so much
that without even trying,
I'll break it again.

PHOTOSHOPPING MY SISTER'S MUGSHOT

I crop out the trailer and the splintered remains of the front door.
I crop out your name all over the news.
I crop out the sawed-off shotgun they found hidden in the yard.
I crop out the blood-vacant faces of every soul who was sold to.
I crop out their family's hunted hearts.

I rotate the image until you are upside down, hanging
from the monkey bars, hollering my name, *Andrea, look what I can do!*
I zoom in until there is no lighter beneath the spoon, just ice cream
dripping from your face, and me trying to teach you
how to blow out the candles the day you turned two years old,
your cheeks—pink balloons giggling away gravity.

I give more detail to the background. I pose you
beside our bloodline, our grandfather throwing his liver
through the kitchen window, our grandmother on her knees
sweeping up the glass. I zoom in to the pieces she didn't find.
I find them in the sole of your shoes on your worst day of junior high.

There is a thin line between skewing the truth
and giving a panoramic view. I don't know if I'm widening the lens
or just making an excuse when I say that you were a kid
the first time you used. You wanted blue hair
and a boyfriend, not a conscience

that wouldn't have a good vein left, not an abscess
in the arm you would one day not hold your family with, not me
falling off the wagon of my unforgiveness,
running to the police station, begging them
to replace your mugshot with the negative,
your dark side in full light,

the filth-hungry scream in your body every time you tried
to get clean, the clinic that told our mother you would die
if she didn't send you back out to the streets
to find the poison, to kill the bugs,
how I'd count your legs when you walked into a room.

How I still do. But that isn't the right exposure.
Because you were also the kindest person I ever knew.
And that in itself has been its own dark room
considering the ugliness is to scale,
considering our family tree

and how there isn't a person who loves you
who isn't dead on the branch.
How loving you less might have been the sweetest gift
I could have given my own life, but how that sweetness
would have rotted god's teeth

when every Christmas morning you woke me at 4AM,
more excited for me to open my stocking
than you were to open yours.

How do I say that to a judge
and not sound insane?

How do I say the truth isn't the right filter?
The truth knows nothing
of who you almost were, but I do.
I just click a button. I undo one tiny thing:
    and there you are.

GUARDIAN ANGEL FISH

My love has a prescription for Wellbutrin,
but because I make her happy, she calls me Wellgibson.
I make her happy. Is there anything left to do in this life?
I don't think so. Except maybe adopt a fourth dog, which we both know
she will find, because I pull over when I see a stray,
but she pulls over, learns parkour, scales a building
and pole vaults between rooftops, returning with another
furry bundle, freckling her in fleas.
She also follows me everywhere I go. I don't mind
that it's only to put lids on everything I don't.
What can I say, I'm an open person. So is she.
She doesn't just see people at their best.
She sees people at the best they haven't been yet.
Which is why she loved me long before I loved myself.
Thank goodness I figured that out.
Beating yourself up is never a fair fight.
Those gloves fit no one right, and she always deserved
a me who didn't have to squint through bruised eyes
to see her clearly. And how could I not want to see her
clearly? As she pole dances on the tractor, mows our lawn
in a bikini, rolls out a red carpet to escort the mice back
to pasture, teaches spiders how to weave their webs outside,
and the ants—okay the ants she slaughters with every weapon

she can find, but I forgive her because she forgives everyone
so easily. Watching her do it is like watching paint dry.
There's nothing to see. Everything is just more colorful after.
This morning I was trying to figure out what kind of fish
everyone in our family would be. I asked her
what she would be, and she said, very seriously,
Hold up, let me google the sexiest fish. No, *wait,*
the most beautiful fish. Oh look there's an angel fish!
I am an angel fish! I know there are other fish in the sea,
but there is no one like her anywhere.
She minds her own business. Changes her mind
as often as she needs to. And she never lies,
which irritates me because she also edits my poems.
Can't keep that look off her face when I use adverbs.
I don't know how she can expect me to not write the word *beautifully*
while she's sitting beside me? But *beautifully* doesn't bug her
nearly as much as *honestly*, which I honestly begin half of my sentences
with—and she's worried that suggests the other half of what I say
is a lie. But here's what I figured out: I am a liar. I lie all of the time.
The other day I said, *We will all have to say goodbye sometime.*
That wasn't true. Saul Williams was right when he wrote,
Only believers in death will die. I don't believe anything can take me
away from her, nor would I want it to. But it wasn't always like this.
There were countless times we were more flammable than instagrammable,
though we were creative about it. Spent an entire summer arguing
via badminton so we could drive the birdie of blame at each other's skulls.
I was gonna leave that out of this. But this isn't only for us. It's for everyone

we can convince not to wait for a tragedy to stop calling it zero-zero
when it could so easily be love serving love. I had no idea how much
would change when all that mattered became all that mattered.
These days our biggest argument happens on our daily walks
near the lake. I always want to walk back the same way,
which she doesn't enjoy. *I like a circle*, she says. We can't agree
because I want to do it all again, see it from another angle.
The back of the coffee line when she didn't know me
but told me I was ordering the wrong drink. The back of my hand
where I first wrote her name so I could remember her birthday
when we were still friends. The back of her arms where she tattooed
the longitude and latitude of where we first danced. The birds flying
backward back to the cold just like her racing home from her lunch
in the sun when I called to tell her that the doctor spotted something
on the cat scan. When I call cancer the Big C, she is the only one
who knows I mean the big ocean where we met our own Titanic
and didn't sink. She even managed to convince me it was a good idea
for us to dress up as Jack and Rose on Halloween. Though my baldness
was in position to pass up an opportunity to wear a wig, I *was* a bit nervous
to play the part of the guy who dies. But I wasn't really Jack. I was Rose.
And her heart was the door that opened so wide it tore off its hinges
and kept me afloat. Even as I woke up from surgery and asked her
what they found. Anyone who thinks poetry is frivolous has never needed
someone to tell them something unspeakably hard, beautifully.
My guardian angel. My guardian angel fish. I will never not be
swimming beside you. Just like I will never be done writing this love letter.
For which this is only the prologue, Baby. I've barely begun.

MAGA HAT IN THE CHEMO ROOM

There is a man wearing a MAGA hat in the chemo room. I can't get a good look at him because my body is plugged into a bunch of beeping machines, but Meg just tore the headphones out of my ears and whisper-screamed, "There is a man wearing a MAGA hat here!"

I misplaced a medical marijuana edible around 3AM last night and couldn't find it until I woke up, chugged the glass of water beside my bed, and noticed the water tasted *weird*. So I am relaxed in public for the first time in my entire life. My thoughts are snuggled between stacks of jelly doughnut pancakes. I am right now pouring syrup over my frontal lobe, which is to say I'm chill today. Chill and terribly terribly terribly disturbed. Who wears a Trump hat to chemotherapy!? Why didn't this guy get the memo I got?! The one that said "don't wear political attire to chemo"!? Who sent me that memo? I sent it to myself. Why did I do that? I have no idea.

Every article of clothing I own rocks a political slogan. March For Our Lives, Rest In Peace Patriarchy, Black Lives Matter, Queerdo. My own sister makes hats with the E crossed out of the word HATE to spell simply HAT and I'm not even wearing that. When did "don't hate people" become too edgy of a statement for me to make? Have I become a coward? Did my radical hysterectomy make me less radical? Has facing my own mortality robbed me of my politics?

I see a Trump hat and think, "When that person dies he's not gonna be a ghost. He's gonna be a white sheet." I see a Trump hat and think, "When I die, dude's gonna show up to my funeral waving a *god hates queers* sign at my family's tears." That is—if he knows I'm queer. I suppose there's a chance he thinks I'm straight? That I'm bald now but in a healthier year I'm rocking a blonde bob with face-framing highlights. That I'm a mascara model who only temporarily used up my wishes. That I'm wearing this blush to sunkiss my already peachy cheeks—not because my red blood cells have been devoured by radioactive vampires and I look dead without it. Who wears a Trump hat to chemotherapy? Trump lost his right to tweet. Pigeons have more permission to lead the country.

In the chair closest to mine there is another man who isn't wearing a hat, but who I'd guess is a Trump voter because he's just mentioned to the nurse that he owns *a few Mercedes*. I know democrats who own a few Mercedes—I just bet they mention it less in rooms full of strangers fighting for their lives. The first rule of being a rich liberal: act like you don't have money. Be so down to earth you're actually dirty. No one can pull that look off Bernie. Everyone can see that Bernie is genuinely into conserving water. And shampoo.

I wish I could say my hairdo is an environmental decision. A sacrifice I made for mother earth. Because something to know about me—I am convicted in my convictions. I believe in my beliefs. I have very strong opinions about my very strong opinions. So strong that when folks say I can't take my politics to the afterlife with me, I think, "Well, that's not true." Because my politics aren't my politics. My politics are my soul. I'm not going anywhere without my soul. And that guy's politics aren't his soul. I don't think souls have machine gun collections.

That guy's politics are more like his fist or his incisors or his spit. I want to tell him, "You can't take your spit to the afterlife with you. Not even to hell." But he doesn't think he's going to hell. He thinks I am. He doesn't know I'm going to heaven just to see Jesus standing outside the pearly gates with a sign that says GAYS NOT WELCOME, and God in the clouds above him laughing like an ethereal 6th grader, saying, "We're just kidding! Look, we made the pearly gates rainbow just for you! Look, we made chips and hummus!"

"Oh my god," I'd say, "how'd you know queers love chips and hummus!?"
"Because I'm god!"
"Oh my god, is it true you're letting all the nonbinary folks in first!?"
"Yes!"
"Oh my god! That's why you call it the holy trinity and not the holy binary, isn't it!?"

Here's what's true—I don't wear political attire to chemo because I desperately want this room to be a country where no one looks at me and identifies me as their enemy. I want to feel what I rarely feel outside of here—that everyone is rooting for me to survive. Even MAGA hat guy. I want him to want me to live so long I could walk over to him right now, tell him I had to have my ovaries removed, and he'd be so kind, he'd say, "Andrea, you can totally have one of mine."

There is a land *that* free somewhere. We just think believing in it is a child's prayer, something you only let yourself want when you don't yet know this world. But if that land can't exist in this room where everyone is being told they could die soon—how will it ever happen out there where everyone thinks they have so much time to kill, to slaughter?

Mercedes guy has a daughter who loves him. I can see it in his eyes. And MAGA hat man has an angst inside of him I recognize from everytime I had a pain so deep I thought peace was shallow and blame was the only way to dig it out. That kind of digging hurts like hell. It's the opposite of living—hoarding ideas that are so wrong they chase the soul out of the body that believes them. I've been without my soul before. When you're there you stop seeing anything as it really is. You think you know everything and you can't be convinced you don't.

Something I don't know right now—I don't know if I'm gonna keep coming here week after week. I'm going to see these guys week after week after week. And then one week I won't. Their chairs will be empty. And I'll have no words for the feelings inside of me. I'll only have tears that I will struggle and struggle to explain to anyone outside of this place because everything in my politics knows the middle ground is where this earth will go to die. But when anyone in this room leaves this world, part of me does too. I feel it in every cell of me now—that I am not a *me*. I am one eyelash on the eyes of humanity holding on for dear dear life trying to get the eyelashes beside me to look in the right direction before are all wiped off the face of this planet that desperately wants us to live of natural causes like kindness, like caring, like knowing our bodies are clothes we are all growing out of so quickly. And one day we will be only souls who can see we always wanted the exact same wish to come true. I know we will understand that when we leave this world. The planet is just so desperate for us to know it now too.

WELLNESS CHECK

In any moment,
on any given day,
I can measure
my wellness
by this question:

Is my attention on loving,
or is my attention on
who isn't loving me?

IN THE CHEMO ROOM, I WEAR MITTENS MADE OF ICE SO I DON'T LOSE MY FINGERNAILS. BUT I TOOK A RISK TODAY TO WRITE THIS DOWN.

Whenever I spend the day crying,
my friends tell me I look high. Good grief,

they finally understand me.
Even when the arena is empty, I thank god

for the shots I miss. If you ever catch me
only thanking god for the shots I make,

remind me I'm not thanking god. Remind me
all my prayers were answered

the moment I started praying
for what I already have.

Jenny says when people ask if she's out of the woods,
she tells them she'll never be out of the woods,

says there is something lovely about the woods.
I know how to build a survival shelter

from fallen tree branches, packed mud,
and pulled moss. I could survive forever

on death alone. Wasn't it death that taught me
to stop measuring my lifespan by length,

but by width? Do you know how many beautiful things
can be seen in a single second? How you can blow up

a second like a balloon and fit infinity inside of it?
I'm infinite, I know, but I still have a measly wrinkle

collection compared to my end goal. I *would love*
to be a before picture, I think, as I look in the mirror

and mistake my head for the moon. My dark
thoughts are almost always 238,856 miles away

from me believing them. I *love this life*,
I whisper into my doctor's stethoscope

so she can hear my heart. My heart, an heirloom
I didn't inherit until I thought I could die.

Why did I go so long believing I owed the world
my disappointment? Why did I want to take

the world by storm when I could have taken it
by sunshine, by rosewater, by the cactus flowers

on the side of the road where I broke down?
I'm not about to waste more time

spinning stories about how much time
I'm owed, but there is a man

who is usually here, who isn't today.
I don't know if he's still alive. I just know

his wife was made of so much hope
she looked like a firework above his chair.

Will the afterlife be harder if I remember
the people I love, or forget them?

Either way, please let me remember.

SPIDER

All of my pain is a spider
I've learned not to crush
with the heel of my shoe

but to guide with a page
of my journal
into an empty glass.

I ask questions about
its life, its purpose
as I walk careful

out to the garden and rest
it down on the earth.
My pain—how happy

it is to leave me
whenever I treat it
kind.

TINCTURE

Imagine, when a human dies,
the soul misses the body, actually grieves
the loss of its hands and all
they could hold. Misses the throat closing
shy reading out loud on the first day of school.
Imagine the soul misses the stubbed toe,
the loose tooth, the funny bone. The soul still asks, *Why*
does the funny bone do that? It's just weird.
Imagine the soul misses the thirsty garden cheeks
watered by grief. Misses how the body could sleep
through a dream. What else can sleep through a dream?
What else can laugh? What else can wrinkle
the smile's autograph? Imagine the soul misses each falling
eyelash waiting to be a wish. Misses the wrist
screaming away the blade. The soul misses the lisp,
the stutter, the limp. The soul misses the holy bruise
blue from that army of blood rushing to the wound's side.
When a human dies, the soul searches the universe
for something blushing, something shaking
in the cold, something that scars, sweeps
the universe for patience worn thin,
the last nerve fighting for its life, the voice box
aching to be heard. The soul misses the way

the body would hold another body and not be two bodies
but one pleading god doubled in grace.
The soul misses how the mind told the body,
You have fallen from grace. And the body said,
Erase every scripture that doesn't have a pulse.
There isn't a single page in the bible that can wince,
that can clumsy, that can freckle, that can hunger.
Imagine the soul misses hunger, emptiness,
rage, the fist that was never taught to curl—curled,
the teeth that were never taught to clench—clenched,
the body that was never taught to make love—made love
like a hungry ghost digging its way out of the grave.
The soul misses the unforever of old age, the skin
that no longer fits. The soul misses every single day
the body was sick, the *now* it forced, the *here*
it built from the fever. Fever is how the body prays,
how it burns and begs for another average day.
The soul misses the legs creaking
up the stairs, misses the fear that climbed
up the vocal cords to curse the wheelchair.
The soul misses what the body could not let go—
what else could hold on that tightly to everything?
What else could see hear the chain of a swingset
and fall to its knees? What else could touch
a screen door and taste lemonade?
What else could come back from a war
and not come back? But still try to live? Still try

to lullaby? When a human dies the soul moves
through the universe trying to describe how a body trembles
when it's lost, softens when it's safe, how a wound would heal
given nothing but time. Do you understand? Nothing in space can
imagine it. No comet, no nebula, no ray of light
can fathom the landscape of awe, the heat of shame.
The fingertips pulling the first gray hair
and throwing it away. *I can't imagine it,*
the stars say. *Tell us again about goosebumps.*
Tell us again about pain.

INSTEAD OF DEPRESSION

try calling it hibernation.
Imagine the darkness is a cave
in which you will be nurtured
by doing absolutely nothing.
Hibernating animals don't even dream.
It's okay if you can't imagine
Spring. Sleep through the alarm
of the world. Name your hopelessness
a quiet hollow, a place you go
to heal, a den you dug,
Sweetheart, instead
of a grave.

HOW THE WORST DAY OF MY LIFE BECAME THE BEST

"When you are trapped in a nightmare, your motivation to awaken will be so much greater than that of someone caught up in a relatively pleasant dream."—Eckhart Tolle

When I realized the storm
was inevitable, I made it
my medicine.

Took two snowflakes
on the tongue in the morning,
two snowflakes on the tongue
by noon.

There were no side effects.
Only sound effects. Reverb
added to my lifespan,
an echo that asked—

What part of your life's record is skipping?

What wound is on repeat?

Have you done everything

you can to break
out of that
groove?

By nighttime, I was intimate
with the difference
between tying my laces
and tuning the string section

of my shoes, made a symphony of walking
away from everything that did not
want my life
to sing.

Felt a love for myself so consistent
metronomes tried to copyright
my heartbeat.

Finally understood I am the conductor
of my own life and will be even after I die.
I, like the trees, will decide what I become:

Porch swing?
Church pew?

An envelope that must be licked
to be closed?

Kinky choice, but

I didn't close.

I opened
And opened

until I could imagine the pain
was the sensation of my spirit
not breaking,

that my mind was a parachute
that could always open
in time,
that I could wear my heart
on my sleeve and never grow
out of that shirt.

That every falling leaf is a tiny kite
with a string too small to see, held
by the part of me in charge
of making beauty
out of grief.

ALL THE GOOD IN YOU

When all the good in you
starts arguing with all the bad in you
about who you really are,
never let the bad in you
make the better case.

BOBBY LEFEBRE

Laureate 2019–2023

BOBBY LEFEBRE fuses a nontraditional, multi-hyphenated professional identity to empower communities; construct new realities; advance arts and culture; and serve as an agent of provocation, transformation, equity, and social change. LeFebre is a decorated artist and cultural leader working cross-sector and cross-discipline to activate radical imagination and progressive pragmatism for social good. Holding a bachelor's degree in psychology from the Metropolitan State University of Denver and a master's degree in art, literature, and culture from the University of Denver, LeFebre is a Fellow of the National Association of Latino Arts and Cultures Leadership Institute, the National Association of Latino Arts and Cultures Advocacy Institute, and the Intercultural Leadership Institute.

LeFebre was named Colorado Theater Person of the Year in 2019, a National Catalyst for Change Fellow in 2020, and an Academy of American Poets Poet Laureate Fellow in 2021. In a contemporary literary landscape marked by systemic biases, LeFebre has elected to diverge from conventional industry trajectories. Rather than pursuing validation through traditional publishing avenues, he's opted to engage poetry in experiential contexts. Though LeFebre has never once sought publication, the Emmy-nominated writer's work has been featured by the American Academy of Poets; in *The New York Times*, *The Huffington Post*, *The Guardian*, and *American Theatre Magazine*; and on NPR. Poetry has taken LeFebre to forty-eight states, thirteen countries, thousands of stages, and countless hearts. His work has been featured on radio and on TV, and a room has been named for LeFebre at the Denver Foundation's Casa Grande on Poets Row.

Through writing and performance, I continue the legacy of the oral tradition like a humble and righteous heir, proud of my inheritance and anxious to carve out my own territory. I explore, celebrate, and critique the human condition and spirit by constructing narratives of justified indignation, academic insight, and barrio analysis. The poet, when effective, is a cultural worker. A healer. A conductor and conduit of a world begging us to see and celebrate our relationship to it. The poet is more than a writer. The poet is more than literature. The poet is a cultural translator. A humble prophet. A communal visionary. A dreamer and a realist inseparably entwined. The poet manifests, evokes, and makes tangible the visions and love that live within us all. Good poets raise the consciousness of our collective psyche, heal where there is hurt, celebrate where there is joy, share where there is space, disrupt where there is stagnation, build where there is opportunity, and challenge where there is complacency. These philosophies guided my service as Colorado poet laureate. As Colorado's ninth poet laureate, I had the honor of participating in hundreds of events, readings, cultural gatherings, and conversations across the diverse and vibrant state of Colorado and beyond. From the sweeping landscapes of the Western Slope to the familiar streets of Denver and the quiet beauty of the San Luis Valley, I had the opportunity to connect with people far and wide. So many communities, homes, spaces of worship, libraries, cultural spaces, social actions, and more invited me in and welcomed me with open arms; I am profoundly grateful for the warm embrace of that collective spirit. Many shared with me that, prior to my appointment, they didn't even know Colorado had a poet laureate. Being the youngest and first Colorado poet laureate of color was both an honor and a stark reminder of how far we have left to go.

My term was not without its challenges, particularly as we navigated the uncharted waters of the COVID-19 pandemic. Yet, in the face of adversity, poets are known for resilience and adaptability. We leveraged technology to bridge gaps imposed by physical distancing, bringing poetry and the power of words to people. Through virtual readings, online workshops, and social media interactions, we found new ways to connect, inspire, and heal. We were reminded that artists are first responders. That words are indestructible bridges connecting us across the social, political, cultural, and psychological borders we impose upon one another. As a person with Colorado roots since time immemorial, serving as Colorado poet laureate was more than a title; it was a calling, a duty, and one of the greatest privileges of my life. I am proud of how I wore the laurels during my tenure, and I know my people are proud of me too. We made this shit fun and cool. It will be poets of all kinds who usher us into a more just world. Until we get there, and then after.

~Con Safos.

—BOBBY LEFEBRE

FIELDS

Grandpa Rodriguez was a stargazer. An observational astronomer. Un cosmólogo de campo who slept in a toolshed in the lettuce fields of California, the potato fields of Colorado. El viejo techo de madera invited the Milky Way to peek through its cracks at midnight. My grandfather, I imagine, while lying on his bed of hay, would contemplate the constellations. Admire Cuauhtli's celestial wings and dream of flying away. When he would tell me these stories, I swear I could smell pesticides on his breath.

My grandfather was a campesino. A migrant farmworker. He toiled in soiled clothing, bent in the heat of an unforgiving sun tending to a pregnant earth. Callused hands and a tender heart. The Mexica taught us that our current age, the Fifth Sun, would only be birthed by self-sacrifice. By self-immolation. In some ways, I guess, I too am a Fifth Sun. My grandfather leaped into the sun so that I could dig my hands into the soil of my family history, and instead of lettuce, harvest these words.

INTERVIEW

The reporter interviewing me
refers to me as "Chicano poet"
and I do not flinch
She asks me what I think
about umbrella terms

Latino?
"I'm cool with it"
Latinx?
"I'm cool with it"
Latine?
"I'm cool with it"

When she asks me why,
I speak of vastness

I tell her that only a fool
cannot see that waves are the ocean too

SANTUARIO

In the land of my forefathers,
the sun kisses the piñon trees so tenderly
they glimmer emerald in the distance.

The earth and the chile are red.
The adobe has become a caricature of itself.
Turquoise gags as the white woman fetishizes the neo-colonial theft around her neck.

Wilfred runs a cantina.
He asks me about myself and then talks shit;
we laugh and drink in his time capsule in Chimayo.

The bar is bare, but lived in.
A broken jukebox collects dust like a broken heart.
He says "god bless you" as we leave.

I still take my hat off upon entering every capilla.
Ignore the holy water beckoning me from the font.
I can't tell you the last time I convinced my fingers to make the sign of the cross.

The retablo upon the altar is beautiful.
The colors of colonization always pop.
There is a war inside my blood.

The struggle of land and language and people and politics
as pronounced as the smile
that also always seems to bring me to tears.

The doors entering the Santuario at Chimayo
are heavy and made of wood.
Heavy and made of wood like a cross.

A cross holding the crucified hangs upon the altar.
The altar is intricately painted and is made of wood.
Wood is also what the pews were carved from.

In the pews, there is an elder clutching a crucifix.
59 beads rotating with purpose between pointer-finger and thumb.
The Lord's Prayer leaves his lips rhythmically in Spanish like a song.

The echo of his baritone bounces across the thick, cold adobe.
His eyes are sealed shut. Sealed shut as if he is trying to see something.
Sealed shut as if he is trying to forget.

Faith is a beautiful paradox.
The way it professes certainty without proof.
The way it suggests flight without wings.

I watch the fearing genuflect and braid their hands into willful submission.
I watch them root their ritual in elemental things:
water, fire, dirt; all things you can see.

Faith hangs from the hearts of men
like an aberrant piece of art I admire from afar
but could never get myself to buy.

How beautiful it is to browse.
Appreciation dripping from my heart like
the wax of the holy spirit burning upon the tabernacle.

CHILE

After the cosecha
when the sun retires
and the chile is firm
and the stems taut—
gather a bushel and enjoy the aroma abounding.

Grab a spool of twine
some scissors
play music that reminds you of home
take a seat
and ready your fingers.

It is possible
you will see your grandfather's hands
in yours
The wrinkles—valleys
veins—rivers.

Though he is long-gone
you may hear his voice say,
"tie a slip-knot primero, así."

You will grab three chiles in your left hand
and wrap the knot
around the taut stems
pulling till it's tight.

You will wrap more twine
around the three chiles;
four times to be exact—
create another loop
then tighten.

Repeat this process
until you have ten groups
of three chiles on each string;
until you see generations unborn
readying their fingers
to tie knots the way we do.

TAMALES

The sun has yet to open its eyes
yet mom is in the kitchen kneading masa.
The manteca glows iridescent on her fingers
as we talk about life and laugh at even more trivial things.
Marvin Gaye is playing in the background;
mom sings with a smile.

I gather the hojas that are soft from soaking overnight
and ready the carne that has patiently bathed
in red chile for two days.
Although, at this point, I could do this with my eyes closed,
I take in mom's instruction as though it is the first time.
"Make sure the hojas are silky side up," she says.

I continue. There is nothing quick about this process.
Ritual is never rushed. Tradition takes generations to mold.
Prayer is always conducted with purpose.
What is god, but Corn Mother resting in your hand?
What is heaven, but your maker bestowing creation stories
onto you as you root yourself in a future that vows to never forget its past.

TORTILLA

In San Anto, the flour tortillas are always warm, fluffy, and fresh.

Comal kisses color quemaditas onto their celestial surface
so artful, creator claps from afar.

The corn evangelists decry the perfect white moons as a curse of the colonizer,
but the dance on the hyphen between Mexican and American, between North
    and South,
has always been a toe-tap across a line whose sole purpose was to divide.

My Lyft driver speaks to me in code-mixed Spanglish, a primary language
    shared by those birthed
in Nepantla—there is no such thing as living in-between,
no such thing is ni de aquí, ni de allá, only simultaneity—
two things, many things existing, here, and now, at the same time.

"It's early, pero los breakfast tacos are a must, que no?"

Inside, an accordion-heavy tune plays on the jukebox. Something dramatic
and sad in Spanish about a man whose woman found another lover.

Nobody has ever been wronged by a flour tortilla.
They will never betray you for corn.
If that isn't love, I don't know what is.

MAGIC

When my grandfather returned from work, he would place his lunchbox on the mustard-colored vintage Maytag dishwasher, find my grandmother and kiss her three times on the lips saying, "*te quiero mucho, vieja!*" He often left traces of sawdust on her blouse from his day's work at the carpentry factory.

One Wednesday, as my grandfather and I sat on the sofa, he asked me to pull the old photo album off the shelf. Together, we flipped through family photos. He introduced me to distant relatives, showed me the place he was born, and ended by holding a picture of himself in a coffin at his own funeral.

Suddenly, my grandfather's words morphed into an hourglass. The sand descended as he began to gather into a small pile of sawdust next to me. My grandmother came into the living room and asked, "who gave you permission to look through the old photo book?" I told her abuelo said it was ok. She looked at the pile of sawdust sitting next to me. Pausing for a long moment, wearing a mischievous smile, she said, "fine. But you tell your grandpa whenever he returns, I am upset he came home without giving me my three kisses."

SPANGLISH

The man in Mexico City
selling me tacos
can smell that I'm not from around here.

The Rs rolling off my tongue
stagger clumsy
like a baby learning to walk—
my verb-tense confusion
creates a car crash
in the middle of our conversation.

"¿No eres Mexicano, verdad?"
he asks as he scoops *al pastor* into fresh corn *tortillas.*
"Si, pero de allá,"
I reply with loaded reservation.
"Mexicano-Americano."

With confused eyes he asks,
"¿Entonces, porqué no hablas bien el Español?"

And I want to tell him
about the time my grandfather came home from school,
purple and blue shiner glowing like watercolor paint upon his café con leche skin,

blood drawn by a bully's fist running red down his nose
asking his mother in Spanish why she made him Mexican
and if he could change his name to something that rolled off the white kids'
    tongues a little bit easier,
and why the fresh burritos he took for lunch
couldn't be sandwiches on white bread instead
and why the teacher always slapped the back of his head
when he talked to the other brown boys
in the only language his grandfather prayed in,
and I want to tell him about my parents
who bound and gagged the Spanish language,
holding it like a hostage in the trunks of their tongue;
an attempt to spare us the degradation of the past,
and I want to tell him more
about the man standing in front of him,
about the multi-generational fight for dignity,
the freedom of rearming oneself
with the language and culture of their past,
how education and forgiveness can eradicate shame,
how we are brothers separated by a colonial languages and false borders,
how they tried to teach us we have different blood
running through the same veins,
how the eagle and the nopal are tattooed into my heart as they are his.

But there is a long line of people behind me,
my tacos would get cold,
and my sentences would travel broken

like a drunk man stumbling home
from a hollow night at the bar.

I simply answer him,
"es una historia largo."
He corrects:
"*Larga. Es una larga historia*,"
as I smile and walk away.

FRIDA

The fine-ass ruca at the red light
in the car next to me
rocks sharp eyebrows that resemble
two blackbirds in flight.

She's eating a burrito, texting,
and has tattoos scribbled across her body;
the kind the homeboy does in the living room for practice or a pint or a case.

Keith Sweat is blaring from her speakers.
She sings as though she wrote the shit.
"I will never do anything to hurt you . . . . . . I'll give all my love to you."
I turn my head, smile, and nod.
"What you know about this!?"
she asks with enthusiasm, and then speeds away.

I see her hoopty has no plates and there's a pig creepin' three cars back in the
rear-view.

I switch lanes and trail her to block
the squad car's view of her infraction,
singing the hook to the song a cappella,

"And if you need me baby, I'll come running"
She makes a right and heads off into the afternoon like a song.

ADVICE

They invite me to a thing
where the men in suits all look the same
and they twirl and clink wine glasses
as the cheese sits next to the olives
on plates too small to hold anything but image—
everyone is secretly starving—
and they laugh at each other's jokes
even though they are not funny
and they talk about golf and last quarter's returns
and they ask me to read something
that is joyful and festive and celebratory
something inspiring that will make people feel good about gathering,
but 50 migrants just died in a truck at the border
and the Supreme Court is an active shooter
and the police filled another Black man with 60 holes
and I am not a topical poet
but the elders have taught us that the job of an artist is to reflect the times,
so I get on that stage
and I do what I do the only way I know how
and when I am done
someone tells me *the position of Poet Laureate is supposed to be apolitical*
and I say, *"maybe it is, but I am not,"*

and sometimes, the only thing better than a standing ovation
is a room full of silence.

A mentor once told me
sometimes your job as an artist
is to be invited somewhere
and ensure they never invite you back

DOGS

The new people in my neighborhood walk their dogs off leash at the park a block away from my house where there are signs that say you must keep your dog on a leash. Code enforcers and cops roll by, even smiling and waving sometimes, because, man, *aren't those little rescued mutts cute*!?

Meanwhile, on the neighborhood app, Nextdoor, these same people who walk their dogs off leash where there are signs that say you must keep your dog in a leash, gripe about the unhoused man who camps along the south end of the park. They mention the man's presence is an "*eyesore*"—reminding the good people of the internet that it is illegal to camp in a park.

It is 6AM and a police officer is talking to the unhoused man camped on the south end of the park. People are walking by and watching the interaction, their dogs loosely running off leash without a care where there are signs that say you must keep your dog on a leash.

NOMAD

The digital nomad
walks into the cafe
with his dog
and MacBook
and he talks about his lifestyle
and how incredible it is
to live somewhere so cheap
with the help of his parents
and the salary he makes
in the United States
and there is a músico playing songs for change
and when he is finished strumming his time-worn guitar
he makes his rounds
with his hat outstretched,
and when he reaches the digital nomad,
he puts not one coin in the hat—
in fact, he shoos him away like a fly—
then the digital nomad
goes back to talking about how nice it is
to live in a place with so much culture
and how he's headed to Chile next
to take some more.

BOOM

This is another poem about how people, children even, are dying at the hands of guns. This is another poem that uses metaphor—a figure of speech that states one thing is another thing. In this case, let's say prayer is policy. If prayer is policy, the connection between prayer and policy is dissonance. Dissonance is a simile. We load it over and over again, like a gun.

I.

The hand tells the gun:
"I am boss."
The gun answers the hand:
"Aim wisely."
The gun tells the bullet:
"Prepare yourself."
The bullet answers the gun:
"I am afraid."
The bullet tells the target:
"I am sorry."
The target answers the bullet:
"I know."
The target tells the blood:
"Don't leave me."
The blood answers the target:

"I must."
The blood asks society:
"How much more of me do you want?"
Society answers the blood:
"……………….."

2.
In the distance prayers ring out:
"God bless the hand."
"God bless the gun."
"God bless the bullet."
"God bless the target."
"God bless the blood."
"God bless the United States of America."

FLORES

When everything
is war

Let love
be a flower

tucked into the barrel
of the gun

BONES

When this body
becomes too weary
to carry the life inside of it,
take the lumber of my remains
and build a shrine.

Of my bones
construct the altar.
Unearth the heirlooms
buried underneath my tongue,
and melt them into glass cylinders.

From my memories,
braid a wick
and light it.
Mix my blood with earth,
sand, and sticks,
mold me into adobe bricks
and let me harden in the sun.
Make walls of me—
use the tattoos from my flesh
to decorate the stucco.

Of my veins,
weave a walkway
that leads to a garden.
Scatter my dust where the roses grow.
Sit with me in times of blooming,
but pluck me like fruit when it is time.

Take my teeth
and place them inside a hollowed gourd.
When you miss my voice,
shake the rattle and dance to my song.
Use clay to make a mold of my lips
and fashion it into a cup you can kiss when you thirst for me.

When you are left with nothing but my organs,
wrap them inside my favorite shirt
and bury me beneath a tree.
As far as my heart,
it has always belonged to you.
Do with it as you wish.

JOSEPH HUTCHISON

Laureate 2014–2019

JOSEPH HUTCHISON is the author of eight full-length poetry collections: *The Undersides of Leaves* (1985), *House of Mirrors* (1992), *Bed of Coals* (1995, selected by Wanda Coleman as winner of the Colorado Poetry Award), *The Rain at Midnight* (2000), *Thread of the Real* (2012), *Marked Men* (2013), *The World As Is: New and Selected Poems, 1972–2015* (2016), and *Under Sleep's New Moon* (2021). He has also published thirteen chapbooks, including the Colorado Governor's Award volume *Shadow-Light* (1982) and a bilingual gathering of his Mexico poems, *Eyes of the Cuervo / Ojos Del Crow* (2018, translations into Spanish by Patricia Herminia, illustrations by Sabina Espinet).

Journals in the US and abroad that have seen Hutchison's poems into print include *American Poetry Review*, *Copper Nickel*, *Edge* (New Zealand), *The Fiddlehead* (Canada), *The Hudson Review*, *The Lampeter Review* (Wales), *The Nation*, *Poetry* (Chicago), *Poetry Australia*, *Poetry Salzburg Review* (Austria), *Prairie Schooner*, and THINK *Journal*.

Hutchison's poetry has appeared in over twenty anthologies, including *A Ritual to Read Together: Poems in Conversation with William Stafford* (2013), *Healing the Divide: Poems of Kindness and Connection* (2019), and *New Poets of the American West* (2010). His work also appears in Ted Kooser's *The Poetry Home Repair Manual: Practical Advice for Beginning Poets* (2005).

Aside from his own writing, Hutchison has coedited three anthologies, including *Malala: Poems for Malala Yousafzai* (2013, all profits benefitting the Malala Fund for girls' education). He also coedits the online journal *Bristlecone*, publishing poetry by writers based in the Mountain West.

Until I served as Colorado poet laureate, although I had published quite a bit, I thought of writing poems as mainly a private activity. I was born and raised in Denver and educated in public schools, and the notion that there is power and truth in writing was instilled in me by three brilliant teachers: Jim Roome, Francis Morrison, and Vernice Van Duzer. It was Mrs. Van Duzer who noticed I was writing outside of class. She lent me her own books and later invited me into a reader's theater group. We edited texts for twenty-five-minute performances. We gave voice to Steinbeck's *The Pearl*, Conrad's *The Lagoon*, and poems by Eliot, Sandburg, Hardy, and MacLeish. Reader's theater taught me that the power of poems flowed from their images and the subtlety of their soundscape.

I went on to study at the University of Northern Colorado in Greeley, where I was inspired by an English professor named Ed Kearns. Ed hosted a group of students in his home one semester, sessions free and free of grades. At the end of our last meeting he handed me a copy of Wallace Stevens's *Selected Poems*. "You won't understand him," he said. "Even the critics may take another hundred years to get him." I've read Stevens for fifty years now and can boast only an imperfect grasp of his work. But I love it, and if I've learned anything it's that poetry should be read first of all for pleasure. Let understanding take its time!

My formal education ended at the University of British Columbia, where I studied with the expatriate Irishman George McWhirter, who has an incomparable ear for language and an eye for students unhealthily obsessed with words. When I left Vancouver, he gifted me one of his books. Part of the inscription read: "Remember—pages are to walk through, not to live in." The best writing advice I've ever received.

Back in Denver, I only now and then performed my scribblings in public, and always in places east of the mountains—north to Fort Collins, south to Pueblo, maybe west to Boulder. I unconsciously developed a mental map of "Colorado poetry" that was limited to the Front Range. Becoming poet laureate gave me the gift of redrawing that map. I traveled all around the state—from Trinidad to Telluride, Fort Morgan to Ignacio, Fruita to Palisade, Durango to Salida—and everywhere I went there were audiences who cared for poetry and accomplished poets previously unknown to me. I was repeatedly struck by how many people in our state see poetry as something not confined to one unit in an English class but an ancient way of feeling and knowing the world that no other kind of writing can provide.

This is why I don't think of our tribe as "state poets." The art is too diverse and dynamic to be defined by borders. On the other hand, our mountains and plains, our communities and their histories, will continue to ground the experiences that color our poems. We'll do what we can to bring it all into words, though we know these landscapes will sometimes elude and always outlast us.

—JOSEPH HUTCHISON

JUNE MORNING

Sunlit room:
a breeze thumbs through
loose papers on the desk.
Shadows of poplars swim slowly on the carpet.
Small lakes on the eastern plains
drink the sky's blue
and reflections of eagles hunt in the depths.
Here, the dreaming grass
flutters in its sleep.
The steady blackbird chatter spouts
out of the flowers.
                                        On days like this
some men long for a God to praise; others
doze in the nameless mountains of the body.

CITY LIMITS

For Melody

You're like wildwood at the edge of a city.
And I'm the city: steam, sirens, a jumble
of lit and unlit windows in the night.

You're the land as it must have been
and will be—before me, after me.
It's your natural openness
I want to enfold me. But then
you'd become city; or you'd hide
away your wildness to save it.

So I stay within limits—city limits,
heart limits. Although, under everything,
I have felt unlimited Earth. Unlimited you.

CROSSING THE RIVER

For Susi

The sky, after last night's wind, is bright
as the eyes of a child who's learned a new song,
and she comes to her father crying, "Listen!"
So he listens. He attends. But it's hard:
to hear what she hears, he must learn to love.

I noticed a woman on the bus one day. A red
birth-shadow flared across her left cheek.
She saw me staring; we each looked down;
the aisle became an impassable river.
If we'd talked? Oh, I'd never have risked
telling her what had first crossed my mind:
"I'll bet it tastes like strawberries."

Strawberries offer their seeds
frankly, not folded away in the core.
My eight-year-old likes them with cream,
a dust of sugar. They taste so good
that she can't keep from singing,
though her cheek's plump with fruit—
which I ought to remind her isn't polite.

But I listen instead. I attend. I am
learning how to hear the beauty she hears
as she sings with her sweet mouth full.

AS THE LATE SEPTEMBER DUSK COMES DOWN

For Brian

In the grassy slush of the fall's
first snow, my son, age three,
is dancing. He's dancing
this boot-heavy jig for joy—
or simply to drive out the ache
of an idle day indoors. He stamps
oblongs in the lumpy whiteness,
now and again gives a shout
made of steam. Then he halts
by the sagging apple tree
and stands a while, head back,
gazing through the ruined fruit,
into the failing light. Sure,
I should call him in. But I want
to savor that glad, forgiving look
that glows on his upturned face.

WALKING OFF A NIGHT OF DRINKING IN EARLY SPRING

For Joe Nigg

Through the budding elm branches, eyes
of traffic lights blink red to green;
the idled traffic surges forward in the dark—

and we stagger on down the alley, joyful,
voices loud and cloudy in the cold.
Where do these hours come from? Hours

when old wounds flare, and the night
opens, and pain boils up into conversation,
as if talk can heal. The sweating bottle

drifts hand to hand, mouth to mouth—
and stars blink through branching clouds,
the blood groping darkly in our heads;

but the moon's here, too. A bright clarity
over cars and streetlamps, over houses
and leaving trees: going with us.

THE BLUE

In memory of Michael Nigg,
April 28, 1969–September 8, 1995

The dream refused me his face.
There was only Mike, turned away;
damp tendrils of hair curled out
from under the ribbed, rolled
brim of a knit ski cap. *He's hiding*

the wound, I thought, and my heart
shrank. Then Mike began to talk—
to *me*, it seemed, though gazing off
at a distant, sunstruck stand of aspen
that blazed against a ragged wall

of pines. His voice flowed like sweet
smoke, or amber Irish whiskey;
or better: a brook littered with colors
torn out of autumn. The syllables
swept by on the surface of his voice—

so many, so swift, I couldn't catch
their meanings . . . yet struggled not
to interrupt, not to ask or plead—
as though distress would be exactly
the wrong emotion. Then a wind

gusted into the aspen grove, turned
its yellows to a blizzard of sparks.
When the first breath of it touched us,
Mike fell silent. Then he stood. I felt
the dream letting go, and called,

"Don't!" Mike flung out his arms,
shouted an answer . . . and each word
shimmered like a hammered bell.
(Too soon the dream would take back
all but their resonance.) The wind

surged. Then Mike leaned into it,
slipped away like a wavering flame.
And all at once I noticed the sky:
its sheer, light-scoured immensity;
the lavish tenderness of its blue.

STRANGE BUT TRUE

The asphalt unrolls out of the gray-dirt
flatness daubed with weeds, two lanes queasy
with August heat. Cranked halfway down,
all the windows shudder. The boy's bare feet,
propped on the dash, bathe in the hot gush
from the open wing (this is before conditioned
air, spring-loaded cupholders, stereo FM).
It's late morning, eighty miles from Dubois,
Wyoming.
                    Father and son left Denver at dawn
to fish the Wind River, where (they both
know) the boy will barely wet his hook
before the boredom takes over . . . his casts
turn sloppy, the snags more frequent; his father
will scold, they'll fight; the boy will end up
in the car alone, sullenly thumbing the lurid
paperback he'd bought for a buck in Cheyenne:
Strange But True.
                              At this moment, though,
peace. The boy can't sleep, but keeps nodding
off into states of suspension; the wind's boom,
the motor's drone, the road's throaty roar
melt and run together in his skull

until his brain's steeped in warm honey;
so that, when his father speaks, the words
float in from far off like sprays of milkweed—
glimmering, buoyant, faintly surprising
(they've driven in silence for over an hour):
"I wonder," he says, "where the rubber goes
that wears off the tires."
                                        A mystery
they ponder for a breath or two—then both
grin, start to laugh . . . until the laughter
floods them with wakefulness, makes
the whole vagueness of Wyoming shift
into focus: flaking highway lines the color
of old mustard, greenish bursts of sage,
phone wires and fences loping by, mountains
thick and blue in the distance . . . and all of it
shining in their watering eyes as they fly—
laughing, father and son—through summer
and the summer of their lives: strange but true.

FREEDOM

The world's just a cramped
space you occupy—all the rest
(so they said) a dream. Freedom
exists, but no one can live there.

As ever, you knew better. So,
when they asked you to don
that cap-and-gown get-up
to collect your family's first

college degree, you told them
no, insisted on no, pretended
not to hear your mom sobbing
in the blue bathroom. Freedom!

And now she's gone, free at last
from pain (they say)—but you
dream of her, hunched over
on the toilet's shag-covered lid,

in that cramped space, leaning
against the vanity with its worn
blue basin and dribbling faucet
none of us could ever shut off.

MCGRATH

I

Of his own pen Heaney wrote, "I'll dig with it."
The same Irish dignity in hard labor pulses
through your *Letter*, enters under the jawline
when we voice your words. Over and over,
reading you, a rush of pure spirit draws
the whole body in—the whole body
politic and mythistorema of the Dream
Americans send their children to bed with.

II

I read you first in self-exile, having fled
the haunted Nixonian darkness, drawn
west and north of your North Dakota childhood,
north of the 49th parallel where, it turned out,
some sanity prevailed.
                                        A bevy of languages
fluttered above the Vancouver streets—
now a Far East chatter like daybreak birds,
now a wood-barrel rumble of Black Sea
wind against the forested Caucasus,
now the British landlady's kindly coos
over milk uncurling in cups of Earl Grey,

now my mentor's Shankill Road lilt
like loops in a Celtic knot.
                                        All this enriched
by your taste for words bristling with history,
maybe half-forgotten but fragrant, invoking
the roots of your urgent and capacious empathies,
your angry love for humanity aching in harness,
the deep-structured rivering of your vision.

III

Vision, as you knew, abides in "the true
road of the spirit," which you sought
and taught yourself to walk. I set foot there
myself years later, and though by then you'd
vanished among its turns, your clear voice
led me. Miraculous, how your vast Letter
kept arriving, healing the rift in me between
self and other. Even now you keep arriving
from the luminous Void, reminding me
what all Earth's creatures hold in common:
this transient *now*—this news that stays news.

THE GULF

The marine biologist sinks
a blue-gloved hand into the Gulf,
then draws it out, stunned silent
by blackness dripping from his fingers.
~~~~~

The columnist and tele-intellectual,
known back in college as Little Georgie,
owl-eyes the moderator and shakes
off the catastrophe. "Accidents happen."
Capitalism's dangerous, he means.
Big rewards demand big risks.
Market wisdom. No pain, no gain.
~~~~~

The heron sails low over the grassy marsh,
legs stockinged up to the knee-joints in crude,
nowhere to land that isn't poison, nowhere
to stand and snap up a clean fish or two.
*

At the edge of the marsh, a half dozen
former fishermen crouch to wipe oil
off the long leaves of grass, in silence;
their Company contracts ban them
from talking to the media. Their pain

has nowhere to land, but keeps on
circling above the beloved waters,
spiraling lower as the weeks go by.
*
Tony Hayward, CEO of BP (two letters
advertised to mean *Beyond Petroleum*),
speaks freely to CNN. "No one," he says,
"wants this thing over more than I do.
I'd like my life back."
                                        Later, he climbs
into a limo that whispers him away
to a throbbing helicopter, thence
to an airstrip where the Company jet
stands ready to loft him back to London,
30,000 feet over the lightless Atlantic.
In his mind he's already holding a tumbler
of Ladybank single malt on the rocks.
How many eleven-thousand-dollar-a-day
paychecks can he "earn" before the Board
cuts him loose?
                              Hell—the sooner the better!
How sweet to sway under a golden parachute,
age 54, the rest of a life in front of him. . . .
~~~~~
Robots on the sandy bottom
saw at the pipe to ready it
for a capping attempt,
~~~~~

but the boil of oil and methane
keeps on thundering up
in diarrheal billows.
A sickening sight, yes—
but far from where we live.
How sad for those living there!
Our thoughts and prayers—etcetera . . .

~ ~ ~ ~ ~

Decaying fish at the fouled tideline—
more fish than Jesus conjured up
at Bethsaida. The Gulf's abundance
wiped out so people like me can drive
twenty-plus miles each way to work,
suckle at bottles of clean spring water,
keep our leftovers chilled for days
before finally tossing them out.

The primordial dead power the pictures
that move me to write, the underwater
cameras that make me an impotent witness.
Even the ink in my pen is implicated,
my better angels beached in slick goop
like pelicans, heads cranked back,
eyes frosted over in the wind.
Even the ink in my pen. . . .

~ ~ ~ ~ ~

Day 46.

TV ads tout BP's commitment to clean-up.
News of a stalled rebound: unemployment, 9.7 percent.

Commercials for the new *Infiniti*: air-conditioned to mimic bucolic breezes;
the dashboard's wood hand-rubbed with silver dust.
The "spill" (a PR term meaning "eruption") stains everything.

Three thousand square miles of the Gulf's surface sheened or slathered, the
Gulf winds infused with stench.

A hundred meters down: the plumes like sprawling Rorschachs, petro-globs
tumbling like fallen angels toward the Dry Tortugas, toward the lightless
Atlantic.

Ocean floor: the very ground of Being a kind of Pompeii, sooted over by rotting
animalcules, most so holy they've never acquired a name.

~ ~ ~ ~ ~

Day 47.

You expected,
maybe,
an epiphany. . . .

~ ~ ~ ~ ~

The Empire once made Greece its suburb.
Then the Empire made the Wild West its suburb.
Now the Empire's made the whole globe its suburb.

Poetry: enslaved to Rhetoric,
or worse, Linguistics.

Whatever you expected
clearly will not come to pass.
Only the Gulf dying as we speak.

Only blackness dripping from our pens.
~ ~ ~ ~ ~
And yet—hypocrite poet!—here you sit,
casting your bitter lines out into the Gulf.
~ ~ ~ ~ ~
Between the I who sneers and the I who grieves,
between the one who writes and the ones who read,
between the solitary heart and nullity: the Gulf.

Against our own greed we side with the Gulf.
Against our pride, our numbed spirits, against
the gag shame has stuffed in our mouths—
we speak out. To restore the Gulf we speak out,
speak to restore, if we can, our own trashed nature.

In a tense not past, present, or future—we speak.
(We speak, said the poet, in the *possible* tense.)

Though our voices may vacillate, we speak
for the "flow of unforeseeable novelty" that is
the Gulf. Using words estranged by politicos,
corporatists, postmodernists, we speak up
for both the Gulf within and the Gulf without—
speaking, anyway, to make the possible possible.

ODE TO SOMETHING

> *Zero does not exist.*
> —VICTOR HUGO, *LES MISÉRABLES*

Why is there something
rather than nothing?
Because nothing
never was, was ever
just a trick of math
that turned
a placeholder
into lack,
into absence—
and zero
like a ball-peen
hailstone
struck
a crack across
the smooth windshield
of speeding
reason, making
the mind's eye see
nothing
everywhere.

But nothing is nothing
like something,

something
with its amber
honeys, cabernets
and cheeses,
blood,
blindworms,
blossoms,
lips, hips, hands,
pain and rage,
heartbreak, night-sweats,
ten thousand joys
intense
and transient.
No wonder
so many dread
the sheer abundance
of something,
its "flow of
unforeseeable
novelty," endless
irruption of
forms and essences.
How can reason hope
to hang its dream
of knowing all
on such a flood?
How feed
its fantasy of mapping

every last height,
every depth, making
both beginning and end
knuckle under
to understanding?
Therefore:
nothing. Nothing
that gives something
direction, an arc
of action,
a story,
a meaning,
the way deities
used to do.

Truth is, though, we
swim in mystery
reason can't (can
never) plumb:
no beyond, only
being and somethingness:
our lives like sparks
in a vast
becoming,
bright flecks
of foam
on a breakneck river,
swirling in the world as is.

SPIRAL PATH

Spira Mirabilis

These white rock chips, raked smooth, make a spiral path
beside the retreat center's garden—a path, the owners say,
good for mind-calming walks. But walking, I wonder:

Did these milky shards come from the canyon's east end
where in these hills our dawns arrive, where the northward
mountainside's long been flayed and scraped? I've watched

machines crawling the gouged scarps like famished insects
out of the early Triassic, year after year unearthing a massive
vacancy, turning the cliff-face into money, into how many

stones under how many feet of how many walkers? (Let it
go. Breathe.) I count my steps. Ignore the blue jay's jeer,
the ground squirrel's chitter and whistle. And the spiral

tightens. I approach the center-point of the path's coiled
watch-spring, touch it, then turn back. A faint breeze.
Pine bough shadows swim on the path like fish in a stream.

*

I walk slower. No end in mind, only the steady side-to-side
of motion, subtle pull of the path's turning. I lean into it,
the shape of its flow. A breath, a breath . . . then out

of some book read ages ago, a grainy gray photo
floats up: an ancient Ligurian quarry above Carrara.
The Roman conquest of that region yielded centuries

of white Luna marble, from which were made their mighty
buildings and statues of Latin gods—all to out-do the Greeks,
whose defeat and subjugation were never enough to ease

the Roman sense of lack in art and religion, mediocrity
that haunted senators and emperors, their minds eaten out
by a ravening hunger and a lust for control. Why else banish

your greatest poet to the Black Sea? Why thrust slaves
into hollow brass bulls and stoke fires under them, treating
dinner guests to their sizzling screams? No surprise then

that thirty-some Roman rulers were murdered in office—
poisoned, stabbed, gutted, fed to dogs . . . only their effigies
propped up at funerals and praised as if alive. Would a spiral

path of rock chips to walk have helped to make them wiser?
Am I any wiser on the spiral path? I can see the end of it
ten feet away, and slow a bit more. Delay, and delay. . . .

*

"Standing still," we say. Yet we can feel the Earth rolling
like a marble in a funnel, in the vortex our middling star
drags behind it: planets, moons, comets, dust . . . flying

through the void at 700 miles per second. No "still point
of the turning world"! Only this leaning into the spiral path,
ache of the effort to drag behind us our personal vortex

teeming with memories, longings, aspirations, regrets:
each life like a quarry in some mountain above Carrara
where we mine such stuff as our little dreams are made on.

CLIFF SWALLOW AT MESA VERDE

Peeow, peeow, peeow, peeow—purrreet!
Each phrase of your swallow-song
ends in praise—for rain-washed sky,
rock-folds, the trickle of springs,
insects delicious on the wing.
Nothing, you insist, to be
gained by stillness . . . so you
take to the windy canyon shadows
high over kivas and cliff-houses,
rise, flutter, dither, swoop—a wide loop
old as the world. Do you remember that girl
under the slanted cave roof, watching you? She
grew, loved, labored, and died watching you.
How many such girls before
the decades of drought, the long diaspora?
How many Anasazi births and deaths while you—
eternal bird—feasted on frantic ants,
cedar beetles, wasps and crickets, and then
lifted away in pursuit of some irresistible cloud?
Escaping your home, age after age, you've wandered,
flying wildly toward the outer edge of time and back
to the nest of this moment—*singing. . . .*

DAVID MASON

Laureate 2010–2014

DAVID MASON'S BOOKS of poems began with *The Buried Houses* (winner of the Nicholas Roerich Poetry Prize), *The Country I Remember* (winner of the Alice Fay Di Castagnola Award), and *Arrivals*. His verse novel, *Ludlow*, was published in 2007 (2nd ed., 2010) and named best poetry book of the year by the *Contemporary Poetry Review* and the National Cowboy and Western Heritage Museum. It was also featured on the *PBS News Hour* and won the Colorado Book Award.

Mason's memoir, *News from the Village*, appeared in 2010. Collections of his essays include *The Poetry of Life and the Life of Poetry* (2000), *Two Minds of a Western Poet* (2011), *Voices, Places* (2018), and *Incarnation and Metamorphosis* (2023). Mason has also coedited several textbooks and anthologies, including *Western Wind: An Introduction to Poetry*, *Rebel Angels: 25 Poets of the New Formalism*, *Twentieth-Century American Poetry*, and *Twentieth-Century American Poetics: Poets on the Art of Poetry*. His poetry, prose, and translations have appeared in such periodicals as *The New Yorker*, *Harper's*, *The Nation*, *The New Republic*, *The New York Times*, *The Wall Street Journal*, *The Times Literary Supplement*, *Poetry*, and *The Hudson Review*. Anthologies include *The Best American Poetry* and *The Penguin Anthology of Twentieth-Century American Poetry*.

He has written opera libretti for composers Lori Laitman and Tom Cipullo. Recent collections of his poetry include *Sea Salt: Poems of a Decade* (2014), *The Sound: New and Selected Poems* (2018), and *Pacific Light* (2022). A former Fulbright Fellow to Greece, Mason taught at Colorado College. He now lives in Tasmania, the island state of Australia.

I remember standing on the capitol steps with Governor Bill Ritter and departing Poet Laureate Mary Crow, looking out on a small gathering of well-wishers and journalists in the vast indifferent thrum of the city. It was a leap into the unknown. I remember Mary's kindness and Governor Ritter's enthusiasm. He leaned close and told me of his affection for the poems of Thomas Hornsby Ferril, especially "Magenta," parts of which he knew by heart. Mrs. Ritter, joining us, told me to "go out there and shake things up." But no one was more shaken than me.

I had pledged to get to all sixty-four counties in the state and do anything I could to support poetry in schools and libraries. In the end I would add correctional facilities, business groups, political gatherings, book clubs, cafes, bookstores, poetry slams—any place where people could be found to listen. While in the end I visited sixty counties, I certainly did not have speaking engagements in all of them. In fact, it was sometimes hard to find people who might answer my email, let alone invite me to their communities. But I found plenty. I remember one Halloween speaking with three strangers in the library of Glenwood Springs. One of them was a librarian, another her spouse, and the third a citizen who had walked in expecting anything but poetry and elected to stay. Then there were gatherings on several campuses of the Colorado Mountain Colleges, where audiences numbered in the hundreds, many of them assigned a book of mine for reading. I learned that an audience of three is as rewarding as an audience of three hundred, and just as important. Poetry moves in many ways, some quiet, some loud. Over the four years of my tenure I gave hundreds of readings and workshops, trying as often as I could to bring other Colorado poets along with me to share the stage. It was easy to get gigs on the Front Range, particularly in Denver and Colorado Springs, but I worked hard to get schools or libraries elsewhere in the state to invite me. Like other laureates,

I did this with a tiny stipend and while holding down a full-time job. My employers at Colorado College were not happy about my absences. Poets have to confront the fact that much of the world finds their efforts unquantifiable. We actually have to count for ourselves.

My laureateship was a joy. It was my opportunity to get to know the state in which I lived—every corner of it, from Fort Morgan to Lamar to the Comanche Grasslands to Trinidad (my father's hometown). I burned up the beautiful miles in my aging Subaru: Alamosa, Durango, Telluride, Ouray, Montrose (where my mother was born), Grand Junction (where she grew up), Craig, Rifle, Aspen, Vail, and Steamboat Springs. Throw in Gunnison, Crested Butte, Leadville, and more tiny towns than I have space to name. In all of them I found people hungry for the life of poetry.

—DAVID MASON

KÉFI

Every meal a communion.
The uninvited dead are here.
Do they miss the taste of wine
or the flickering glare

of the candle in the window?
I remember some of their names.
Their appetites are hollow.
They crowd like moths to the flame

but the poor things cannot burn.
Light-headed in this company,
I look at them all in turn.
The Greeks would call this *kéfi*,

ineffable, weightless, tuned
to the conversations of the night
with or without a moon.
O everything's all right.

It's *kéfi*—coffee would wreck it,
or too much wine, but a song
if I can remember it
will carry us along.

FATHERS AND SONS

Some things, they say,
one should not write about. I tried
to help my father comprehend
the toilet, how one needs
to undo one's belt, to slide
one's trousers down and sit,
but he stubbornly stood
and would not bend his knees.
I tried again
to bend him toward the seat,

and then I laughed
at the absurdity. Fathers and sons.
How he had wiped my bottom
half a century ago, and how
I would repay the favor
if only he would sit.

            Don't you—
he gripped me, trembling, searching for my eyes.
Don't you—but the word
was lost to him. Somewhere
a man of dignity would not be laughed at.

He could not see
it was only the crazy dance
that made me laugh,
trying to make him sit
when he wanted to stand.

STONEWALL GAP

(excerpted from Ludlow: A Verse Novel*)*

Windblown aridity in early spring,
piñon, prickly pear, the struggling scrub.
At noon my shadow pooled beneath my boots,
my eyes surveying ground a step ahead
for arrowheads or any signs of life,
out walking a friend's ranch with Abraham,
the land a maze of dry arroyos, slabs
of pale rock, the flints exposed by weather.

There too the terrible remains of winter,
dead cattle caught in a raging blizzard
lay unthawed in postures of resignation.
I was so intent on treasure that I stumbled
into a ditch and fell across the corpse
of a calf the wild coyotes dined upon,
a gutted leathery thing—it had a face
and I started backwards, stifling a scream.

What was I? Twelve years old? The age I dreamed
Luisa Mole out foraging for water. . . .
On our visits south
I begged to be taken to the mesa country
as if those afternoons on skeletal land
put me in touch with some essential code,

the remnants of a people who moved through,
migrating hunters five millennia past.

Look for a bench, land flat enough to camp on,
a nearby source of water—there you'd find
the silicates in flakes, clear fracture marks
where fletchers made their tools, the midden washed
by wind and flash floods all across the scarp.
Nothing remained in place here. Even trees
had shallow roots. In dustbowl days my father
picked up points by the dozen on this land,

pot-hunting like his neighbors, half in love
with science, more with the electric touch
of hands across receded seas of time.
What had we found? I knew this evidence
of other lives had meaning of some sort.
I saw the strangers, grew among them for years
in my own mind. But was it love or envy?
Was it only pride of place? A kind of theft?

Always looking at the ground beneath my boots,
always listening for the call of Abraham
who'd find a point and let me think I found it,
whose meaty, sun-burnt hands would leave the pool
of wide-brimmed shade, point beyond scarred boots
to the perfect knife, worked like a stone leaf
and left there by the ancient wanderers,
original, aboriginal, and magic.

BRISTLECONE PINE

If wind were wood it might resemble this
fragility and strength, old bark bleeding amber.
Its living parts grow on away from the dead
as we do in our lesser lives. Endurance,
yes, but also a scarred and twisted beauty
we know the way we know our own carved hearts.

SONG OF THE POWERS

Mine, said the stone,
mine is the hour.
I crush the scissors,
such is my power.
Stronger than wishes,
my power, alone.

Mine, said the paper,
mine are the words
that smother the stone
with imagined birds,
reams of them flown
from the mind of the shaper.

Mine said the scissors,
mine all the knives
gashing through paper's
ethereal lives;
nothing's so proper
as tattering wishes.

As stone crushes scissors,
as paper snuffs stone

and scissors cut paper,
all end alone.
So heap up your paper
and scissor your wishes
and uproot the stone
from the top of the hill.
They all end alone
as you will, you will.

HANGMAN

A Big Chief tablet and a Bic
between us on the car's back seat,
the scaffold drawn, and underneath
a code of dashes in a row
for seven letters. Part of a stick-
figure fixed to the noose's O

for every letter missed, until
if I'm not careful my poor guy
will hang with x's for his eyes.
My brother parlays his resource
for big boy words with taunting skill:
"It starts with *d* and rhymes with *force*."

But I don't know the word, don't know
the wet world being slapped away
by wiper blades, or why the day
moved like an old stop-action film
or an interrupted TV show
about a family on the lam.

I let myself be hanged, and learn
a new word whispered out of fear,

though it will be another year
before I feel the house cut loose,
my dangling body and the burn
of shame enclosing like a noose.

COLD FIRE

I

The man about to set the ground on fire
casts an eye to a flicker in a gum tree.
Grandfather. A yellow-throated honeyeater.

His claimed relation, knowledge or mystery,
shames my scientific doubt. His burning brand
purifies with smoke each blade and twig we see,

offers a blessing to every ant at hand,
warns the beetle to move now. *Cold fire coming*.
He says cold fire will creep across the land

and nudge echidna out of her dark homing.
He says the fire is slow but animals should run.
He kneels to earth, half-singing and half-humming.

Grandfather looking on, cold fire will come.
Bow down to the smoke, cold fire will come.

II

Across the ocean in the Ring of Fire
lived a people native to the rain.
The old volcanoes rose up high and higher,

bald snowy domes above the farming plain,
the wet cathedral forest streaked with light
that hardly touched the floor. I'm there again

in soil so deep it seems to build the night
from rotting cedars, chaos of meshed limbs,
the spider webs like filaments of mind.

These are the makings of my native hymns,
my breath clouds nakedly in air like smoke,
cold fire inside me, outside me. It climbs

as the eye climbs on the updraft of the smoke.
My breath is rising like a cloud of smoke.

III

Basalt crystals, like organ pipes in snow.
Snow melted back in wells around each fir
from the body heat of tree, and deep below,

the drum of permafrost began to stir.
The drum would sound when people walked upon it,
a beat of boots among the roots and heather.

And every mountain rose up to its limit.
One could not tell the water from the wind
or from the breath of all that moved within it.

The burn was sunlight where the air grew thin.
The firs hung down their beards of Spanish moss
and hid the winking ruin of a mine.

The glaciers calved in water fresh as loss.
Down through the years came water. Water and loss.

IV

Cold fire discovers as it moves. It is no saint
and martyrs nothing that it touches when it burns
the twigs and bark, leaving a trace of faint

white ash the game and birds will feed upon.
I burn a cold fire here that runs in lines,
a sound like laughter and the hurt that learns.

Cold fire takes and teaches, and it talks in signs
until the fire and smoke are gone. And then it sings.

CUTTINGS

*

Of all the ages of man
or woman, the age of blame
most shrivels the soul—a burnt-
out match forgetting its flame.

*

We condemn
books we have not read,
films we have not seen,
people we have not met,
and feel the injury
of *them*.

*

Two men and a woman
in a room. Who
do you think is doing
the listening?

*

Sometimes you find yourself
in the awkward position
of trying to control the weather.

*

A day without
accomplishment—
by me at least.
At last the rain
comes on, dancing
oh-so-lightly
over the roof,
bringing the change.
*
There used to be always
change in one's pocket.
*
I step out of the house
at night, and a dozen
marsupials run off
to safety in the dark.
No matter how I try
I cannot convince them
that I will do no harm.
*
A day's work:
I moved two lines,
then thought a while before
I cut them.
*

It's like escaping prison,
the frisson of a rhyme.
Let that be the lesson
blessing us in time.
*
Two words kissing.
So many disapprove.
*
Even in this blessed silence
it is so very hard to hear.

ANOTHER THING

Like fossil shells embedded in a stone,
you are an absence, rimmed calligraphy,
a mouthing out of silence, a way to see
beyond the bedroom where you lie alone.
So why not be the vast, antipodal cloud
you soloed under, riven by cold gales?
And why not be the song of diving whales,
why not the plosive surf below the road?

The others are one thing. They know they are.
One compass needle. They have found their way
and navigate by perfect cynosure.
Go wreck yourself once more against the day
and wash up like a bottle on the shore,
lucidity and salt in all you say.

ON THE SHELF

On the kitchen shelf a huntsman spider has left
its skin, which looks so much like itself
I thought twice before touching it. It was still.

The body left and left behind the soul,
feather-light and eight-legged, able to frighten
even when all it wanted was new life.

Perhaps you'll come upon my own shed skins
in houses where my name has been removed,
the habitations I once thought were home,

or find some words of mine in an old book.
I meant them. The words. Every one of them,
but left them on the shelf to go on living.

THE SOUL FOX

For Chrissy, 28 October 2011

My love, the fox is in the yard.
The snow will bear his print a while,
then melt and go, but we who saw
his way of finding out, his night
of seeking, know what we have seen
and are the better for it. *Write.*
Let the white page bear the mark,
then melt with joy upon the dark.

MARY CROW

Laureate 1996–2010

MARY CROW'S TRAVELS shaped her poetry and translation. The poems of *Borders* are rooted in Latin America, where she read the work of women poets for her anthology. Later travel to the former Yugoslavia allowed her to tour that country and write *I Have Tasted the Apple*. Israel residencies inspired poems for her most recent book, *Addicted to the Horizon*. She has also published three chapbooks. Her five translated books are *Woman Who Has Sprouted Wings: Poems by Contemporary Latin American Women Poets, From the Country of Nevermore: Poems by Jorge Teillier, Vertical Poetry: Recent Poems by Roberto Juarroz, Engravings Torn from Insomnia: Poems by Olga Orozco*, and *Vertical Poetry: Last Poems by Roberto Juarroz*. Crow's prizes include Poetry Fellowships from the National Endowment for the Arts and the Colorado Council on the Arts; a Creative Writing Award from Fulbright to read her poems in the former Yugoslavia; a Colorado Book Award; a Translation Award from Columbia University's Translation Center; Fulbright research awards to Chile, Peru, Argentina, and Venezuela; a National Endowment for the Humanities year-long poetics seminar at New York University; and two NEH summer seminars. Her poetry has been nominated some two dozen times for the Pushcart Prize. One of her poetry book translations won a Lannan Award and was a finalist for the PEN USA Translation Award; she was, as a result, invited the following year to join the selection panel for PEN's Translation Award.

Crow has read her poems widely, overseas in France, Israel, Yugoslavia, and Argentina. In the US, she has read at many universities, not only in Colorado but also including the San Francisco State Poetry Center, University of Minnesota, Ohio State University, Old Dominion University, Long Island University, Case

Western Reserve University, Bowling Green University, Wright State University, and Spaulding University (keynote address); at community venues in New York, Tennessee, Ohio, California, Minnesota, Arkansas, Texas, Kansas, Wyoming, and Colorado; and at various sites including the New York Public Library, Word Thursdays, Channel 7 TV, Wisconsin Public Radio, and Aspen Writers Conference.

I served as Colorado poet laureate for fourteen years, from 1996 to 2010, under both Democratic and Republican governors. My principal goal as poet laureate was to increase poetry's visibility in Colorado and to extend acquaintance with Colorado's poetry beyond the state. To achieve this, I traveled throughout Colorado to give readings and workshops both for children and adult communities.

Awarded a grant to expand my work in the schools by the Witter Bynner Foundation, I brought master poets (including Kenneth Koch) to Fort Collins to train graduate students how to teach children to write poems. In one grade school, I paired with a teacher to link poetry and literacy, giving free books to children and providing a reception at semester end so parents could hear their children read their poems. On one such occasion, a father came up to me afterward and told me how much he wished that such a program had existed when he was a child, since his desire to write poems had lacked support.

In addition, I ran a contest for both poems and artworks for posters to be placed on Fort Collins buses in conjunction with the New York City program "Poetry in Motion." Participants in this contest were very excited to have their photos taken with Ray Martinez, then mayor, at a reception for winners in the City Council meeting room; it was heartwarming to see a grade school student artist and a senior citizen poet posing with the mayor as they smiled at the camera. I instituted another contest for local teachers to win prizes for the innovative use of poetry in the classroom, and the nominations came from their students, which the teachers heard read during a reception to honor them. Unfortunately, there were no funds to extend these programs beyond my town, but I did continue to give readings, workshops, and class visits statewide. Finally, I attended national meetings of state poets laureate and was included in the national anthology *An Endless Skyway: Poetry from the State Poets Laureate.*

During these years, I worked full-time on the faculty at Colorado State University and raised funds for many literary readings by both nationally and internationally famous writers, including Nobel Prize in Literature winner Tomas Tranströmer. Among other writers I brought to campus were Carlos Fuentes, Bei Dao, Margaret Walker, Sandra McPherson, Gary Snyder, Adrienne Rich, Richard Hugo, Tomaž Šalamun, Robert Bly, Primus St. John, Linda Hogan, Al Young, Ariel Dorfman, Diane di Prima, Leslie Marmon Silko, Carolyn Forché, Homero Aridjis, Denise Levertov, Simon Ortiz, and Audre Lorde.

My service to poetry and literature included membership on the boards of Associated Writing Programs, the University Press of Colorado, and BkMk Press of the University of Missouri / Kansas City; as president of the Writing Program Directors' Council of AWP; as secretary-treasurer of the American Literary Translators Association; on selection panels of the NEA and NEH; and as director of the Creative Writing Program at Colorado State University.

—MARY CROW

WHAT WAS THAT CITY

After Cavafy

that tangled me in sandy roots, led me
into desert, where I gasped at

vastness and vacancy, pyramids fringing
miles of nothing growing, a void

I vanished into, as imagination gave way
to reality starred with sand, endless beach

where I lost patience with boredom,
with ruins inside me, merciless sand.

Along the river, wrecked temples languished,
doors pouring out a sand-story, above a thousand

buried sphinxes—how small human life looked,
where sky tired of light, where dark seemed

to glow with death's glaring ink, where distant
sand lay like frosted glass, an endless repetition.

I meant travel to set me free, teach me wisdom,
how to bear pain, how to decipher sand patterns.

Instead, each city revealed a hissing resistance
where revenge pitched words like glass shards

between sand barricades—beyond sand,
no end of light. Sky was years ago.

BEYOND TAHRIR

I thought there was more life where
traveling stars hissed rising over desert
or broke through smog above Cairo.

I tried to get lost in crowds
as yellow tanks ground by, body
suspended like a target.

Helmeted police with plastic
shields shouted commands
that splintered in the racket.

Everything in decline—when
was it new? Of course nothing
worked, never had.

Isn't this one form of
resistance? No traveler
unharmed unless too poor.

Even in Tahrir all was gossip,
danger, silence. There were
no maps, no dictionary of the new gestures.

FOREIGN STREETS

I am walking as fast as I can,
shifting my shoulders to slide past
men or the knives of thieves.
And, yes, I need a man,
a man to protect me
from those hot looks on the street
which are hate or lust,
or both. Yes, yes,
I want him to go with me
into the restaurants,
into the streets.
Yes, I admit it:
living alone is dangerous
and I am weary of fear,
weary of clutching
my dusty belongings
under my arms.
Maybe I'm weak
but I'm going to repeat it:
I want a man.
I'm sick of thinking about myself,
of closing my heart
against the day's dozens

of cripples and amputees,
the blind man with festering sores,
the filthy kids who sleep on the streets.

And my anger,
yes that especially:
everyone tells me
everyone is a thief.
Tonight all the corners are filled
with soldiers with their first beards
and machine guns.
I want to slink past.
You won't like my saying it,
but I dream of men
breaking down the glass walls
to get at me,
and the police don't come.
There is so much water.
I wake up crying,

"My child, my child."

ECLIPSED HORIZON

Consider: the extreme
difficulty of the one
solitude, of a perilous
exception who'd make
us happy, consider
the difficulty of
living as though
Mount Atlas were here,
of setting one foot
before the other,
consider how we came
to capture a sense
of direction, gap's
pinch clinching on
slippery sandhills,
consider the difficulty
of securing any river,
horizon's eclipse
sliding toward
mountains, a home
that can engulf us,
the tremendous still
in us somewhere

EVERYTHING IN THE DREAM IS YOU

That's what frightens me—loneliness
ankle deep, Calder's circus,
my racing thoughts, water rising.

Everything in the dream is you.
The pure white canvas, pure black
one, four darks in a red too.

Noise number 12, old sox and doilies—
what a collage you are!
Crickets' hum in a garden scene

also you, and you Pompeii's cattails.
You my American artwork,
cowboy in a Hollywood western.

So if I wake? What do you become?
The brightness of? The curious dog?
Gentle feathering of something's breath.

GETTING READY TO LEAVE FOR SPANISH CLASS, GRANADA, NICARAGUA

A man with a Nike shirt cleans the pool, water gurgling from its sides,
two bathers waiting. Beyond our hotel's open doors, taxis and buses.
Last night at the door our driver shook my hand to show we are friends
and that he is honest though I doubted him when he'd started off in
a wrong direction. Another man sweeps his net through the pool's
water, cobalt from the tiles, net shining too, while the girls fixing
our breakfast smile but pass by, bearing plastic bags. Last night my lover
and I exchanged hot words, and though we never settled our differences,
he lay his head in my lap just before sleep. I know it must be my fault.
No wonder I can forgive him. Neither of us will ever puzzle out
the other. The desk clerk looks bored. I want my breakfast. How can I
study the difference between preterit and imperfect on empty?
The pool has filled with clean water. Unreal blue.

TRYING TO FIND THE WORDS FOR IT

I still don't know how it happened,
but a whirlpool sneaked into every sentence.
Or maybe only a short movie.

Anyway, I didn't see it coming.
Click, and the whole thing went up a notch,
reminding me of bird-thronged cliffs,

of the horizon's brittle edge, map's austerity.
I felt as if I stood before a famous painting—
blurred washes of blue, white, tan—

suggesting water, sky, strips of shore.
Suddenly Plotinus' words came to me:
"the flight of the alone to the Alone."

That is, the precipice on which
a glacier pauses before calving with a boom:
huge chunk plunking into black water.

A steady wind smelled of minerals,
of the ocean floor where old ships dissolve,
leaving only bones, iron bolts, amphorae.

Anyway, at such a moment life appeared dark
as a winter night where a white bird's
blurred flight gave a glimpse of the sublime.

FAULT-FINDING

Even now the ground is slowly shifting
beneath your feet. Even now
zones of weakness are building
behind your back, ready to crack
into fractures. Even now pressures
may exceed the power of rocks
to resist. Think of it:
thousands of fault lace this region.
You live inside a ring of fire
where walls can loom up overnight.
Forces in this landscape
are trying to rearrange your world.
You stand here feeling
you can control nothing,
at any second it is you
who may be heaved up,
and broken.

BLIND SPOTS

December sunlight: the shore of a country
a small boat is shoving away from.

There I lived refining the passive voice,
studying a theory of blind spots.
I wanted to be the one sleep that is knowledge.

Sometimes it happens: you lose almost
everything: waking in the strange room of what you get.

Beyond, a still, flat land.
Winds tumble over fields and river
howling to the sea.

A landscape that seemed something
hallucinated, yet with time became real.

Villages huddle on the shore.
That boat slipping away melts into the horizon
like an optical escape.

Seeing is the extreme courtesy
that arrives when desire dissolves.

Land: still, flat.
You wake and over the bed hangs a picture of twins,
their baby carriage stored in the cellar.

Outside, sigh of the land
a boat is pulling away from.

FACT CHECKING THE BODY

Yes, I know something about the Great Kiss and glass coffin
for the prince. I know something about

the machinery rinsing rocks of silence in this retirement
I've chosen with its nest of a red-tailed

hawk high above where her young lift their open beaks
to insist. But I can't kiss a dead man

awake, not even this prince in blue tunic and gold crown,
not even with words of longing, not even

if I crack through the glass and let raccoons in to lick the coffin
walls with their ripe juices, whatever was left

after an embalming in the style of ancient Egyptians. Did I keep
all the Canopic jars with his organs? My

organs keen with a hawk's thin cry. A sound like muffled
happiness being swallowed. It hurts,

that gnawing. Knowing it takes a long time to get the ruins right.
Loose flesh under upper arms, gratitude

lists, bunion that juts out slowly poking a hole into a shoe.
I didn't petition to live this way, glass coffin

and a prince pale and staring who peers straight through me,
hot days in a rocky space where the sun

grows hotter every year hammering roughness into tomato
and garlic, where the tallest cottonwood

is a green paradise and at its peak, moist pink throats
of baby hawks beg for food.

TRAVEL

In other places other words
name *claws*, *mother*, *transport*.
Or is it that language transforms?
Prague's painted houses in Golden Lane
look like dolls' houses or stage sets.
Spectators jammed the square
when the occupants were pulled out—

Should we put a period to things?
At least the hours chime the same
in every tongue, at least the astronaut flies
as high above every continent of the world.
There she is in that shining capsule
as we glance up with envy.
Don't keep asking me what I think.

We could pull her from space
as if from drowning though she might
prefer to be transported.
And anyway what would it prove?
Primeval forests crowd the hills
above these medieval towns.
Last night I dreamed I was in Prague—

Kafka's "mother with claws"—
and I woke to find myself here,
the castle looming over me,
old city across Charles Bridge,
"Robert the Devil" playing
in the opera house and, at
the Kafka Center, for heaven's sake,
the lunge of Piazzolla's tangos.

CAMPER LOVESEAT

A rainy day, cramped quarters—
so many things to make us
comfortable make us uncomfortable—
dish rack, shifted from counter
to floor and back again, TV,
waste basket and recycle bin—
are we really roughing it?
In the mountains you feel free.

Outside there are no crowds.
No stucco cupids here, no baroque
light glittering mirrors or jewels.
Only empty campsites and picnic
tables, charred wood in firepits.
My nerves are bad this morning.
Unreal, this fear of what? *Speak*
to me. Why do you never speak?

If you get up, we could dress
and eat and walk, we could go
fishing with those tiny minnows.
A hook goes in at the mouth,
out through an eye, just so: watch.

The little fish will be swallowed by
a larger fish, then we'll eat that one.

ARCADES OF WIND

That town in Italy named Carpi, long arcades
around its central square, held no tourists but
me who'd come to view the concentration camp
now slated to reborn as a Peace Retreat when
funds allow. So much desolation. No campaign
to promote this "famous" camp, no billboard
on the outskirts, no anniversary announcement.

I try walking out to the ruined camp, along
a main highway where a car stops to offer me
a ride, no strings of course, only a drink later on. . . .
Still, he drops me at the gate and barbed wire,
long low barracks, row after row of their gray
among waist-high weeds, endless isolation
and in the distance bleaker forest monotony.

2.
Whereas:
desolation proved infinite and people died
here or survived to die in further camps, the huge
pines are innocent and the town, like me, knew
nothing of path-treading between barracks to latrines,
nothing of transport to somewhere-with-no-trace.

Whereas:
nightingales were slaughtered since no
one could scrounge enough to eat in winter.

Whereas:
in this forgotten camp, wind pierces, clouds pursue
each other, then as now, now as then, scene so blank,
even perfect,

Therefore no one invents landscape.

Well, then,
who will plough the wind? Whose descendants
sow discord or harmony? Whose orphan will pace
here after all those promises as he threshes dawn?

UNDER THE CITY

In the huge Roman cistern under Istanbul
a dozen marbles floated in the side walls,
a bust on its side, an upside down plaque
(perhaps from a tomb), walkways echoed
with footsteps till I thought I had arrived
at the Underworld, my steps knocking to
summon the Door Keeper, His Loneliness,
to This Side, lit only by a watery gleam,
wreathing wavering like a movie projector's
afterglow of a blurring sea.

You spoke in that emptiness, stifled in
the circles of your own voice, of how you'd let
slip a river of regret, so much rushing like
a white sail glimpsed in the dimness, *give me
your hands*, in the middle of that eerie theater
where surely some fate awaited us, another pair
of souls wanting to become our souls. *In
the beginning*, I wished to say, *we meant nothing
to each other*, but the sounds that came out were
the seeds of syllables, not syllables of words.

EACH GETS SO SHAMEFULLY LITTLE

Each gets so shamefully little, only half a face, honed to a fine point, like
swallow shadows dipping after mosquitoes, particles like toys shared in a
family, symmetric tools of a mother's mindware, eyelids blinking back tears in
a wavelet analysis, akin to signals from the higher dimensions, spines curved,
space elevated as it unfolds weighted numbers, its arsenal of glibness no
consolation, arsenal of glitches risking wrists and elbows, delicately calibrated
scales of equality, signs of panic where each gets so shamefully little, and
the pull is the pull of gravitas, right arm eased from its socket, introduction
of zero pivoting and bleeding—greeting or goodbye?—hobbled static that
rushes shoulders past the doorkeeper when no one can see a foot in front of
systematic risk

THE MISSING PAGES

He inscribed my copy, *The missing pages*
as well—no explanations, no regrets,
and yet I felt betrayed, by man or fate.

A familiar April sunset, dark-blue
fragments of cloud crowding
an orange sky—is the vast past

really dead, or acting out in our
absent-minded present? When
I opened his diary: so many pages

half-empty. Play of light, frustrations
of weather. Not *think* and *love*,
or *know*, *meet*, *face*. He wrote that

my short hair-cut haloed my face
like zinnia petals, but his poem
seems now to mock skin loosening

from bone, age longer than drought
or rain in his entry log. I count crows
flying overhead, row of minor piano keys.

SCARS

How high can we go?
Shadows at evening rise
to meet us,

above scars (like
skeletons carbonized
in embrace by

lava from Vesuvius)
What is this wind doing
carving blocks of stone

into fat thighs of Venus
we are scaling,
into maws of glaciers,

into the flight

of invisible cities,
empire of repeating ruins

formed in day's
last blaze that strikes
us snowblind

while castle walls
above explode
aluminum mist:

arcades

of zinc, gray plates
grinding as they pull apart—
or did mountain goats

dislodge rocks?—
signals we are nearing—

city, city

of drifting clouds—
a gilded shell of sound
high in air,

wind's home
where mind deserts
the body it has used

POSSIBILITY

And death impossible to remember
while outside some truck groans with its burden
and growls rise and tumble in waves of New Mexican weather
it's fall when tomatoes have to die
and far away glaciers go on crumbling but far
far away, in a plaza Secondo stirs with his shoe shine box

And death's impossible to forget with Bruno
lying dead long ago
gunned down on a street in a tiny town
in Poland where nettles
shove at emptiness
(though Spring is a letter waiting to be delivered)

And death is impossible to remember when friends
sit down at table over pilaf and chicken
and pass around words like vigas or chimeneas
like travels centuries ago
to Khamil kingdom of many towns Marco Polo wrote beside
the great desert of Lop where death is impossible
to forget and flutes isolate the notes
that calm burning fevers leaves go on drying on this patio
into wreaths, and a voice hoarse with agitation

startles Fedya out of reverie where he watched Commandant X
watch the blows of birch rods tattoo his back

And death so impossible
to forget impossible to remember
like borders with checkpoints borders
with tear gas like pillboxes
on the Golan Heights and deserted prisons
in the Negev like the fall of Rome
or Pliny himself talking Latin
in the intervals between pumice-fall and burning gases

between acceleration and deceleration
of a nearby car while the hoarse croak of a bulldozer
talks back to dawn talks back
to death to the impossible to the possible.

THOMAS HORNSBY FERRIL

Laureate 1979–1988

BORN IN DENVER in 1896, Thomas Hornsby Ferril graduated from Colorado College in 1918, after which he served in the Army Signal Corps at the end of World War I. Ferril worked as a technical writer and journalist for much of his life, first as drama critic for *The Denver Times*, then as a filmmaker and writer for the Great Western Sugar Company, where he edited *The Sugar Press*. He also served briefly on the staff of *Harper's Magazine*. Together with his wife, Helen, he edited and published a weekly newspaper, *The Rocky Mountain Herald*, from 1939 to 1972. Several collections of his witty columns for the paper were collected in books. A friend of both Robert Frost and Carl Sandburg, Ferril was highly regarded as a poet throughout the United States, winning numerous awards, including the Robert Frost Medal, *The Nation* Poetry Prize, and the Oscar Blumenthal Prize. He won the Yale Younger Poets award for his first collection of poems, *High Range*. Subsequent collections included *Westering*, *Trial by Time*, and *New and Selected Poems*. Ferril served as Colorado's fifth poet laureate, from 1979 until his death in 1988. His work is notable for its exceptional polish, compassion, and gentle irony, and one of his poems, "Here Is a Land Where Life Is Written in Water," appears in the capitol rotunda in Denver.

NOON

Noon is half the passion of light,
Noon is the middle prairie and the slumber,
The lull of resin weed, the yucca languor,
The wilt of sage at noon is the longest distance
any nostril knows . . .
How far have we come to feel the shade of this tree?

Excerpt from MAGENTA

Once, up in Gilpin County, Colorado,
When a long blue afternoon was standing on end
Like a tombstone sinking into the Rocky Mountains,
I found myself in a town where no one was,
And I noticed an empty woman lying unburied
On a pile of mining machinery over a graveyard.

She was a dressmaker's dummy called Magenta.
I named her that because, all of a sudden,
The peaks turned pink and lavender and purple,
And all the falling houses in the town
Began to smell of rats and pennyroyal.

The town was high and lonely in the mountains;
There was nothing to listen to but the wasting of
The glaciers and a wind that had no trees.
And many houses were gone, only masonry
Of stone foundations tilting over the canyon,
Like hanging gardens where successful rhubarb
Had crossed the kitchen sill and entered the parlor.

NOCTURNE AT NOON—1605

Walk quietly, Coyote,
The practical people are coming now
Into the juniper, into the sage arroyos,
Where the smoke is sweeter than anywhere
And the mud is ready for building
The city of Santa Fé.

While the Puritans over in England
Are getting ready to whisper,
There is a way and we will build a ship,
People in motion are looking at the sage
And seeing where the yellow goes in August
In all the violet sage and silver sage
Along the Rio Grande,
Not that they need the yellow on a faring,
But knowing where it is
And what hills are behind it,
As gulls know where an ochre billow beats
On something that is rock.

Coyote, on the silver road of Spain,
Stalk in the noon, the little mice are dozing,
While you are panting, evening comes to Spain,

Darkens the sculptured rats in Tarragona,
Closes the last Sevillian marigold,
Blackens the windows in Our Lady of the Sea,
And the sailors' sheds grow dim in Barcelona.

Be soft, Coyote of the noon,
Far to the east here is an evening that
Is more than many nights:
This evening, for the first time in the world,
Will Shakespeare leads a madman to his heath
Against the wisdom of a patient fool;
This evening, for the first time in the world,
The little hoofs of Don Quixote's nag
Start striking fire from flinty roads of Spain,
A little trot today, some salty grass,
The first star and the last pale cloud are set.
The cloud is over England, Lear is ebbing
Into the northern lightning of the air;
Somewhere there is a storm, my Sancho Panza;
The star is sinking in the Rio Grande,
Where Cradle Flower with teeth white as a beaver's
Laughs at her lover, Medicine of Corn,
Weaving his body through a hoop of osier.

NOTED

I have finished winter nearly,
Secretary to the stalks,
Wild blue lettuce, kinghead, yucca,
Sagebrush where my red mare walks.
Noted: sundown hurts a man,
Noted: planets fixed and frozen,
Noted: meeting on the plain
A dead man's cousin.
Noted: magpies need a glade,
Noted: by the time you touch
Any twig or grama blade
You have changed that much.
Noted of a cottonwood:
Hate could crack you down,
War is ever twice as near
As the nearest town;
Noted of a cottonwood:
Love can hold you ever,
Noted: willows tillering
From the frozen river.

BEYOND WHAT RANGES?

Tell me, beyond what ranges of the reasonable will
Does faring of a city quest?

I ask you this in Denver, Colorado,
Lip of the bulldozer against the skull,
Churning the dead to furrows of new exile,
Numb as the pistons when the diesels cool
And the steel crane nods
A dragline sag
Down the sandpit pools of evening.

They say a child was drowned today in a sandpit.

I near remember how it used to be
The very morning of this very day:
These pools of sandpit water were not here;
Instead there towered a high and yellow bluff
Yucca-dry as the spiney blink of a horned-toad;
The bluff sheered back ten cottonwood shadows from
The bake of the raw-hide shrink of the river bed;
Gophers, cactus, chattering cater-cousin,
Strawberry runners of the buffalo grass
Clamping the powdered herd songs of far cattle,

Every root in place and nothing trembling
But a whisp of dusty whirlwind spiraling off
Like a girl-child losing a tune she nearly danced to.

How came these waters deep so suddenly?
How was the great bluff moiled, unsocketed
And cast against the skyline of the sky,
Oracular mortar webbed of steel and dripping
To stiffen on the trestles of the westwind
Over the lintels of lightning?

They say a child was drowned today in a sandpit.
Who was the child?
Where did her people come from?

ALWAYS BEGIN WHERE YOU ARE

Always begin right here where you are
And work out from here:
If adrift, feel the feel of the oar in the oarlock first,
If saddling a horse let your right knee slug
The belly of the horse like an uppercut,
Then cinch his suck,
Then mount and ride away
To any dream deserving the sensible world.

HERE IS A LAND WHERE LIFE IS WRITTEN IN WATER

Texts for the murals by Allen T. True in the rotunda of the Colorado State Capitol Building

INTRODUCTORY SONNET

HERE is a land where life is written in water,
The West is where the water was and is,
Father and son of old, mother and daughter,
Following rivers up immensities
Of range and desert, thirsting the sundown ever,
Crossing a hill to climb a hill still drier,
Naming tonight a city by some river
A different name from last night's camping fire.

Look to the green within the mountain cup,
Look to the prairie parched for water lack,
Look to the sun that pulls the oceans up,
Look to the cloud that gives the oceans back,
Look to your heart and may your wisdom grow
To power of lightning and to peace of snow.

First panel: Indian worshiping rain

Men shall behold the water in the sky
And count the seasons by the living grasses.

Second panel: fur trappers led by water

Then shall the river namers track the sunset,
Singing the long song to the Shining Mountains.

Third panel: the wagon people reaching water

Here shall the melting peaks renew the oxen,
Here firewood is and here shall men build cities.

Fourth panel: gold released by water

Water shall sluice the gold yellow as leaves
That fall from silver trees on silent hills.

Fifth panel: the desert farmed by water

And men shall fashion glaciers into greenness
And harvest April rivers in the autumn.

Sixth panel: the engineers bring water to the cities

Deep in the earth where roots of willows drank
Shall aqueducts be laid to nourish cities.

Seventh panel: electric power from water power

Water the lightning gave shall give back lightning
And men shall store the lightning for their use.

Eighth panel: for the future

Beyond the sundown is tomorrow's wisdom,
Today is going to be long long ago.

MILFORD E. SHIELDS

Laureate 1954–1975

BORN IN JASPER, IOWA, on October 9, 1898, Milford E. Shields moved with his family to Montrose in 1905. He attended local schools, and after graduating from Olathe High School he began working for a farming operation in the area. In the fall of 1920, Shields married Nellie Myers, and the couple moved to Durango, where the poet began a thirty-four-year career as a movie projectionist, first at the Rialto Theater and later at the Kiva. Shields also served as editor of the Durango Herald's poetry column, "Singing San Juan." By the time he retired in 1978, Shields had curated more than 1,200 poetry columns for the paper. His own poetry was published in three collections: *Colorado and Other Poems* (1943), *Burning Weeds and Other Poems* (1945), and *Static Land* (1949). In 1954, Colorado Governor Daniel Thornton named Shields to the position of Colorado poet laureate. In that capacity, Shields sought to foster international goodwill by writing poems to famous figures around the world. He also composed poems for the dedication of the United States Air Force Academy in Colorado Springs (1954) and the centennial celebration for Fort Lewis (1978). The poem Shields wrote for the latter event is displayed in a bronze plaque on the Fort Lewis College campus. Milford E. Shields served as Colorado poet laureate until 1975, and he died on February 19, 1979.

SAN JUAN BASIN

The sky precipitates its hue—
The farther higher blue on blue—
The deepening shades blend swiftly down,
Fuse outer mountains into crown,
Then racing in more vivid sheen
They grow into a sea of green.

San Juan puts on the springtime's choicest form:
The quick of dawn, the morning's irised warm;
She draws bright blossoms from conceptions pure
And veils their perfume in the clinging breeze;
She choirs the birds and then attunes the trees—
In summer loveliness completes her lure.

The sea of Eden is so virgin fair
That sun and sky stoop to the presence rare,
A high clear warmth is in the atmosphere
As mystic nuptial spins a vapor here.

A brilliancy buoys on the stirring mist
Where earth and heaven have embraced and kissed.
And hopes and joys and ecstasies here dance
Upon the substance of the circumstance.

They swell to farther higher blue
Where perfect sky completes the hue.

THESE THINGS ARE FREE

These things are free:
God and love, and poetry.

God is the author and the light
Unmeasured and unweighed;
Most priceless thing in cosmic flight.
On it no price is laid
For God is free.

Love is the consciousness of light,
The language of the thing;
This heart's companionate delight
Is joy for serf and king,
For love is free.

And poetry is song of light,
Unmeasured and unweighed,
The lyric of the soul's delight
Inherited, not made,
For poetry is free.

These things are free:
God, and love, and poetry.

FLOWERING CLOUD

A cloud was flowering overhead,
White petals on the earth were shed.

The snow dissolved and was as rain
Which was distilled to dew again.

A honeysuckle budded there
And blossomed vapor to the air.

COYOTE

He shuttles through the dusty, silent sage
And moves along the subtle avenues;
Intangible his tracks from age to age,
Immutable the course that he pursues.

He passes through the spaces vague and vast,
And sways to the monotony of light;
In voiceless patience is his cadence cast,
In day's depression keeps he drabish blight.

When night dissolves the last restraining bars
He shakes off dust, and in his dignity
He lifts unfathomed eyes to bolder stars;
He draws high breath and in it he is free.

He feels the bursting of an ageless urge,
And he barks out a sharp, unmeasured cry;
The native voices of his earth there surge
As coyote calls to the indulgent sky.

MARGARET CLYDE ROBERTSON

Laureate 1952–1954

BORN MARGARET CLYDE APPLEGATE in Indiana in 1870, she graduated high school in Kansas. Her first marriage to George Ellsworth ended in divorce, after which she moved to Colorado in 1890. She married mining engineer William Earl Robertson in 1897. They lived in Leadville, where she sang light opera and wrote. She signed her published poems as Clyde Robertson. Her books included *They Rise Accusing*, *Fool's Gold*, *The Yellow Witch*, and *The Legend of the Kissing Camels*. Robertson was in her eighties when, in 1952, she was appointed Colorado's third poet laureate, a position in which she served until her death in 1954. Often comic, her poetry displays a flair for earthy drama and story.

TALK O' THE TOWN

Young Poney Nelson,
    The talk o' the town,
Gadding the streets
In a scarlet gown;
Too good looking
To be a nice girl,
Hair all frowzed
In a coppery curl,
Swishing ladies,
Chins in the air,
Pass up Poney
With a stony stare.

Upper-crust crowd,
With a family tree,
Driving home
In the evening see
Young Poney Nelson,
At half past ten,
Loafing on the corner,
Talking to the men.

Got no money
And got no folks,
Blew into camp
With some mining blokes.
Sings like a bird
On a maple bough;
Any old tune—
Don't care how,
Don't care what,
And don't care when,
Puckers up her lips
To please the men.

Trips like a fawn
On the dance hall floor;
Pert Poney Nelson
Has partners galore.
Young dames whisper
And old dames glare,
Young bucks whistle
And old bucks swear.
Singing and dancing,
The talk o' the town,
Pert Poney Nelson
In a scarlet gown.

Years won't loiter
And youth won't stay;

Young Poney Nelson,
Old and gray,
Hobbles the streets
Of the mining town
Trailing the dirt
With her tattered gown.

Potter's grave
On a windy hill
Got her at last.
She left a will
Naming the men
To carry her there;
Naming the parson
To make the prayer.
Each man wearing,
To shrive his soul,
A blood-red rose
In his buttonhole.

Scions, three,
Of a family tree;
Nothing to do
They all agree!
Judge and Banker,
Parson and Bloke,
Rose pinned on
Each funeral cloak,

Pace down the aisle
With pious frown.

Old Poney Nelson,
The talk o' the town,
Rides with the four
To the windy hill!
Three men wondering
How they'll still
Storms a-brewing
With three old brides
Waiting to tan
Their sinful hides.

Guilty and trembling,
Mum as a clam,
Only the Bloke—
Didn't give a damn—
Gallantly laid
A lily crown
On old Poney Nelson,
The talk o' the town.

LEN B., TIMEKEEPER

A funny chap was old Len B.
    Every day the camp could see
His flappin' legs march down the street,
Right foot—left foot—on the beat
Of twelve o'clock to get his grub.

"All things gotta go on time,"
Old Len B. said, "like a rhyme."
Ruther 'lowed he oughta know,
He could fiddle and he could blow
A right smart tune on the cornet.

And that wan't all! He led the band,
When Mike O'Reilly wan't on hand.
Old Len B. had great respect
For laws laid down by the elect
Who lived way back in "the good old days."

"Hitchin' tunes," he called jazz.
Got right mad when they used to razz
Him. "Messin' up time'll be the curse
Of the whole dodgasted universe,"
Len B. said, and the boys just laffed.

Stomped the beat for loose-toed dancers,
When he called the good old lancers.
"Sun and moon and stars go round
'Cordin' to God's time, which is sound.
Don't double up yer step there, boys,

"Don't get gay with the universe;
Speedin' up time'll make things worse."
Most made Len B. sick abed
To see time changin' so, he said.
Everything syncopatin' round.

Kept up till some son-of-a-gun
Went to monkeyin' with the sun.
Set it up an hour ahead
O' where it oughta be, old Len said.
Sent his protest to Washington.

Wan't no use. The sun kept shinin'
All outa time, Len said, pinin'
Till just a month to the very day
The clocks was changed he passed away.
Len B. 'lowed his time was done
When fools got monkeyin' with the sun.

GOLD RUSH

Leadville was mad as Babylon.
  There's gold in the hills! On an on,
The tale ran swift as a forest fire.
Wenches for sale! Wantons for hire!
Gold in the hills! A pick or pan
And luck in the lap of every man.

On to Leadville! Over the Pass
Where the glaring snow is hard as glass.
Swear and sweat and cheat and hate,
Gamble and guzzle, lust and mate.

On to Leadville! Bunk in a shack
On a pile of rags and a gunny sack
Two miles high in freezing air.
Grab a claim or grubstake where
Men at dawn are muck at night,
Blown to hell by dynamite.

TIMBERLINE

"The trail goes up
    And the trail comes down"—
The old man sang
Then paused to poke
The dying log
Until the smoke
Wreathed and wreathed
In wisps that twine
Like crooked trees
At Timberline.

"The trail goes up
And the trail comes down"—
The old man crooned
And swayed his head
Like a weary branch
On a wind-blown bed,
Tossing, tossing
Tufts of pine
Tethered to earth
At Timberline.

"The trail goes up
And the trail comes down"—
The old man nodded
Like a leaf,
A shriveled thing
Stayed for a brief

And lonely hour
Upon the vine
To dream of hills
At Timberline.

TIN CUP

Tin Cup Town
    Is tucked between
The giant hills
Where pine trees screen
The clawing rocks
With kindly grace.
If you ask me why
The name of the place
I can only tell
The tale to you
The Old Timer told
And swore was true.

The name itself
Sounds harmless enough
And the Old Timer didn't
Seem so tough;
But of all the yarns
Of greed and gold
His was the grimmest
Ever told.

We had killed a quart
Of rotten juice
And the old man's tongue
Was wagging loose.
I had but a bare
Half hour to stay
Before the stage coach
Passed that way.
It was getting dark,
But we sat down
And he told me the tale
Of Tin Cup Town.

"Sure, young feller,"
The old man said,
"And I bet yer eyes
Blug outa yer head
And yer belly squirms
'Fore I get through
Tellin' some things
I know ter you.

Now, mind you,
What I say, I say,
And my meanin's clear
As the light o' day:
There's blue in silver,

Brown in lead,
Green in copper,
But gold is red;
Redder'n blood
In a miner's pan—
But talkin' together,
Man to man,
Would you shoot a rat
If you seen one there
Crawlin' outa that crack
By yer chair?"

I reached for a drink
And gulped it down.
"Old Man, we're talking
Of Tin Cup Town."
"You're right, young feller,
But diggin' fer stones
Sometimes you dig up
A dead man's bones."

Suddenly, from
A hill near by,
Came a prowling
Coyote's cry;
Then it died away
And all was still.

"As I was a sayin'
Me and Bill,"
He rambled on,
"We drifted in
'Bout the same time;
Had no tin—
Nothin'—but
The duds on our back.
We bunked together
In this old shack
And started in
Prospectin' round
And it wa'n't long
Before we found
Good pickin's in
A shaller hole.
But we never told
A cussed soul;
Just panned the dust.
And piled it up
Waitin' to paralyze
Old Tin Cup;
Plannin' as how
We'd do it brown—
Go on a bust—
Shoot up the town.
Lousy millionaires

Out on a spree—
Lemon pie
And licker free."

"Hold on, Old Timer,
Let's get this straight;
Was the camp named then?
It's getting late
And the stage goes down
But once a day."

"Young feller,
What I say, I say,
But there's some things
I ain't never said
And there ain't no tales
Told by the dead.
There's blue in silver,
Brown in lead,
Green in copper,
But gold is red;
Redder'n blood
In a miner's pan."

The sing-song words
Through his whole yarn ran.
Some way I didn't like his face;

And I didn't like the feel of the place.
A chill came through
The crack in the floor
And I edged closer
To the door.

"Thar's me and Bill
And a yaller dame
All mixed up
In Tip Cup's name;
The dame blowed in
About the time
Things was goin'
Big at the mine.
Me and Bill
Was young bucks then
Sportin' round,
Like other men,
And the dame she tuck
A shine to me.
So I brung her here
To the shack—we three
Workin' together.
Then, one day,
And mind you,
What I say, I say,
Her and Bill

Wa'n't seen no more;
But I swear they never
Went outa that door.

Whar they planted the gold,
I never knew;
But that crack in the floor
Whar the cold comes through—
Well—there's some things
I ain't never said.
And there ain't no tales
Told by the dead."

I took one leap
And struck the ground
And I never stopped
To look around,
Just ran like a white-head
Down the trail.
I had missed the stage
But I'd heard the tale.
But I said to myself,
And you'll say the same,
How in hell *did* Tin Cup
Get its name.

NELLIE BURGET MILLER

Laureate 1923–1952

BORN NELLIE BURGET in Iowa in 1875, she graduated high school at age fifteen and earned a BS degree from Upper Iowa University in 1894. With her husband, Lucas A. Miller, a doctor, she moved to Colorado Springs in 1908. In 1923 she was named Colorado's second poet laureate, serving until her death in 1952. Her poetry often arose from spiritual and metaphysical experiences. Miller founded the Colorado Springs Poetry Fellowship in 1943 and remained an active member for the rest of her life. Her books included *In Earthen Bowls*, *Pictures from the Plains and Other Poems*, and *The Sun Drops Red*, her collected poems.

QUESTION

Will you tell me, Mistress April,
How the spring comes on
In a certain little town
I know?
Do not tell me it is backward there,
And slow!

Is it green along the river?
Have they fixed the water-gap
And does the old mill grind?
Do the children find hepaticas, still,
On the shady side of Walker's hill?

Are the gardens plowed
And the plum-trees popped out white?
Do the lilacs bud?
And the Robins call for rain
In a trickling tune, half joy
And more than half pain,
In the waning light?

Is there still somewhere
A breath of burning brush

Upon the air?
And does the lazy Dusk
Come trailing across the pasture-lot
With a start in her hair?

A MORNING IN AN OLD LIBRARY

The sun has been very busy all the morning
Setting bright new patches on the old gray walls
With diligence unscriptural;
Running curious fingers
Over dingy rows of well-worn books
Looking for dust;
Pointing scornfully
At certain upstart volumes,
Prinking garishly
In red and purple petticoats,
Shocking the staid respectability
Of the best old families;
Coaxing mellow tones of green and amber
From dim tapestries
And lighting up the frayed and faded rugs
With unexpected crimson;
Lingering approvingly
Upon the sentimental faces of an old-time print;
Peering officiously
Within the cushioned depths of rusty leather chair,
To catch some idle dreamer
Napping there.

Very busy in the corner of a dusty pane
Drones a boisterous drunken fly,
Wakened prematurely,
Tippling gloriously
On the rare sweet wine of April
Reeling shamelessly,—
Shade of Omar,
With your jug beneath the vine,
Beware!

I, too, am busy in my quiet corner,
Like a gray old spider spinning
Long-drawn threads of silken words;
Like a crafty spider weaving
Curious webs of interlacing thought,
Just to make a snare
For some radiant passing fancy—
Hope to catch it unaware.
Faint sweet musty odor of rare old yellow volumes
Mixed with breath of drifting plum-bloom
In the air;
Guilty sense of something else I should be doing
Round the house somewhere,
Making joyous dalliance
Doubly fair!

I HAVE LOVED HOMELY THINGS

I have loved homely things,
The scent of fresh-dried linen, and the warm earth
After rain;
The sight of a hollyhock, freshly-crimson,
Outside the pane.

I have loved quiet things,
Slow-moving shadows of the windmill's fingers
Above the well at noon;
And drowsy murmur of three cottonwoods
Gaunt against the moon.

I have loved small things,
Moist sticky fingers of baby-hands
Within my own;
And under my feet three stumbling puppies,
Clumsy and overgrown.

Mansions are for the city-bred,
But for country-folks like me,
God keeps a cottage with hollyhocks,
A child, a well, and a tree,
And a kitten or two, maybe.

PAGAN IN CHURCH

The sermon was tedious that day, without doubt,
And a tipsy bee on the window-sill
Tumbled and droned, incessantly.
But still I cannot quite make out
How I came to float on a southern sea
With a drunken rollicking pirate crew
From out of a strictly orthodox pew.

Call it fancy, if you will,
Or the ghost of a long-dead memory,
Or lay it all on that sodden bee.

I sailed all day on a sea of glass
Where the sun laughed through a sky of brass—
Then shipwreck came—and heaven grew
Slowly from out two eyes of blue.
My dear, was it you
That I found on the shore?
Then why the cross
And the bloody stone?
What gruesome deed must I atone?

Such a safe straight path I am walking now,
But what if the saint with the placid brow
And the scholarly drone,
Could know how my pagan soul flies far
To a wind-swept hill 'neath a southern star
And clings to a cross
In the night alone,
Or gashes its breast
With a knife of stone?

You daintily settle your sleeve's soft lace,
And find the hymn with a deft sweet grace,
Looking at me with accusing face;
Caught me napping, again, you see,
Parson is closing his final *fifthly*,
Out of the window darts buccaneer bee.

MASKS

Life is a mask that we wear
To cover up our hopeless face,
Our dull and puzzled stare;
Lest friend or foe should come upon us unaware,
Should sudden come and see and know
The things Life hides
And that they hurt us so!

Death is a mask that we wear
To veil the gladness of that quiet grace
And dim the radiance falling fair;
Lest friend or foe should look upon us lying there,
Should start and look again, then whisper low,
The *thing Life hid,*
That Death had wooed us so!

AN ASTRONOMER MUSES

To the memory of Camille Flammarion

So, Mars has gone his way again, unheeding all our signals;
We have been so vigilant, so neighborly for naught.
No doubt the fiery planet is unfit for life—at least
A life intelligent as ours . . .
Let's see what's happening now in China—
That's nearer home:
Three thousand killed,
A city burned—

Fools, to fight about a crumb
Upon a dungheap, while your earth is whirled
On cosmic journey through expectant stars!
To them our trenches where men died in writhing heaps
Seem but the pin-scratch which some careless child
Traced on a mirror's silver face . . .
What to these speeding stars is Austerlitz?
Can they find Caesar's ashes with a telescope,
Or tell where sleeps the Corsican?

Talk with Mars?
It is quite possible that Mars gave up the quest
About the time that we were grinding down sharp stones
To supplement our knotted clubs in keeping peace.

Perhaps they said, "The earth is desolate,
Or held by some inglorious race
Whose dull eyes never seek the stars."

Honk, honk,
My neighbor grows impatient while his wife
Applies the rouge once more upon her wrinkled cheeks;
They will miss the rising of the curtain.

Honk, honk,—
My neighbor has not seen the stars in many years.
His eyes are fixed upon the busy street,
And ledger's crowded page;
At night he seeks some brightly-lighted place
To pass the time—
Time!
I could fancy that the dead moon laughed.
My neighbor does not know there is no time within these silent voids
I look upon each night—only eternity.

To one, if there be one upon the nearest star,
Musing alone, as I do here tonight,
This little earth we think so precious to the universe
May be invisible . . .
And yet we dare to say that God himself came down
To die for us upon a tree!

The church-bells chime,
The Dawn steals in on chilly feet,
The Morning-Star looks down benignantly
On worlds that come to birth and worlds that come to die.
So she smiled on Thebes, on Galilee,
On gladiators waking to a Roman Holiday.

The church-bells chime—'tis early Mass
And now the patient priest will call God down
To fill the bread and wine—
Not my God—not *mine!*
My sowe of the Stars could never be so small.

And yet, I *wonder*—
Wildest fancies have a grain of truth stuck in the sieve,
And idle dreamers without lens or text
Best science to the fact sometimes;
They leap from the shores of the seen with mocking laughter;
Pulling after them the invisible thread,
They leave a clue—we but follow after.

I know there is a law that binds the whole,
Some day we'll find and name it;
A subtle heart-beat, pulsing throughout space,
Which is not light, nor heat, nor yet the swift white flame
We've harnessed to our use.
When we do find it, we shall know
It has been with us always,

Unregarded . . .
What if it should be just *love*,
God's love, supporting circling suns, and holding safe
The sparrow in its flight?
God's warm enshrouding love that knows no great nor small—
Why, then, the madmen beat us to it after all!

Ah well, the white flame waited while we made our tallow dips,
And Love must wait its hour!
Mars shall swing on his returning spiral many times,
Unheedful, before the slender thread thrown by the Nazarene
Shall harden into filaments of steel
Safe for the multitude to cross . . .

It is a dream—
But dreams have turned to facts before our wondering eyes
before . . .
I must have sleep—
I maunder;
This way madness lies.

ALICE POLK HILL

Laureate 1919–1921

BORN IN KENTUCKY in 1845, Hill attended the Science Hill Female Academy, an all-girls school. In 1872 she moved with her husband and son to Denver, where they ran a dry goods store. All her life, Hill was active in the Denver arts community, teaching music and writing poetry. She founded a Shakespeare study club for women, and, in 1881, a literary group called the Round Table, serving as its president for twenty-five years. She was also involved in founding the Denver Women's Club and the Denver Woman's Press Club. Other memberships that kept her active socially included the Colorado Historical Society, the Daughters of the American Revolution, Daughters of the Confederacy, League of American Pen Workers, and the Poetry Society of Colorado. Her books included *Tales of the Colorado Pioneers* and *Colorado Pioneers in Picture and Story*. It was she who lobbied then-Governor Oliver Henry Shoup to create a state poet laureate position. He named her to the post in 1919, and she served until her death in 1921.

CHRISTMAS HYMN

The angel voices of the sky
Which on that holy night
Sang, "Glory be to God on High"—
Still sing of joy and light.

That light, whose clear and shining beam
Illum'ed the shepherd boy
And led to Him whose love supreme
Supplants all fear with joy.

O, light divine, be ever near;
Let not thy rays grow dim,
Till we, like shepherds, without fear,
Through faith are led to him.

TO ALICE—MY NAMESAKE

Fair, joyous child, with wondrous eyes,
The royal purple 'round thee lies,
Love's scepter strong is in thy hand,
Subjects are e'er at thy command.

No arrow-word has pierced thy heart,
No faithless friend caused tears to start,
Thy senses have not felt the pain
Of anxious waiting all in vain.

Time fast or slow thy soul knows not,
Thy smiles, thy tears are soon forgot.
No heavy thoughts yet cloud thy eyes,
Thy stream of life reflects the skies.

Look at me now, in happy mood,
Which seems to whisper, "All is good."

Yes, all is good; truth early sown!
'Twill light thy way when youth has flown.
Dear, happy child, our queen thou art!
Those rosy lips, with smile apart,
I stoop to kiss; their touch is sweet

To loving lips that with them meet.

Queen may'st thou reign in future years,
Love-crowned like Esther 'midst thy peers
Conquer all foes within, without,
Until "Well done!" the angels shout.

I AM NOT READY YET

In the nursery was burning a fire, warm and bright,
And the lamp from above threw a radiant light,
On a little boy's head with its soft curling locks,
He was busily building his houses of blocks.
There was joy in his heart and a smile in his eye,
And unheeded the fast flying moments went by.
"It is late," said his papa, "you must go to bed."
With a face full of sorrow he looked up and said:
"O papa, I am not ready yet.
"See my house is not finished, Oh, please let me stay."
He again sadly pleaded when going away:
"O papa, I am not ready yet."
And thus often we see in the nursery of life,
Busy man so intent upon pleasure or strife,
That he stops not to think as the years hurry by,
There's a time here to live, and a time yet to die.
Building houses on earth, building castles in air,
'Tis but little he recks, there's a time, too, for prayer;
But when called to the slumber which closes his days,
With his work all unfinished he earnestly prays,
"O Father, I am not ready yet;
For my soul I've neglected, I thought not of death."
And he sadly implores with his last fleeting breath:
"O Father, I am not ready yet."

ACKNOWLEDGMENTS

The Editorial Committee (Andrea Gibson, Bobby LeFebre, Joseph Hutchison, David Mason, Mary Crow) would like to thank the many people and organizations who helped to make this book a reality. Thank you first and foremost to Turner Wyatt for starting us off and guiding us along the way. Thank you to Julia Seldin for putting the manuscript together and meeting with us as we all consulted and did what was necessary to meet deadlines. Our gratitude for their financial support goes to Colorado Creative Industries, The Denver Foundation, Let's Choose Love Foundation, Academy of American Poets, and the many individuals who donated to our project. Thank you to Bonfils-Stanton Foundation and Colorado Creative Industries for supporting our public events. Thank you to

Hayley Kirkman and Superfunc Studio for designing our book cover and doing an amazing job managing our marketing efforts. Thanks to the Andrea Gibson Poetry team for stepping in after Andrea's passing.

Thank you to the Center for Literary Publishing and University Press of Colorado for publishing our anthology.

CREDITS

ANDREA GIBSON

"Acceptance Speech After Setting the World Record in Goosebumps" (in a slightly different form), "How the Worst Day of My Life Became the Best," "Instead of Depression," and "Wellness Check" from *You Better Be Lightning* by Andrea Gibson (© 2021.) Courtesy of Button Publishing, 2021.

"All the Good in You," "Photoshopping My Sister's Mugshot," and "Tincture" from *Lord of the Butterflies* by Andrea Gibson (© 2018.) Courtesy of Button Publishing, 2018.

"In the chemo room, I wear mittens made of ice so I don't lose my fingernails. But I took a risk today to write this down," from Poem-a-Day (Academy of American Poets, May 30, 2023). Used by permission of the author.

JOSEPH HUTCHISON

"As the Late September Dusk Comes Down," "The Blue," "City Limits," "The Gulf," "June Morning," "Crossing the River," "Ode to Something," "Strange But True," and "Walking Off a Night of Drinking in Early Spring" from *The World As Is: New and Selected Poems, 1972–2015* by Joseph Hutchison (NYQ Books, 2016). Used by permission.

"Cliff Swallow at Mesa Verde" from the chapbook *Cliff Swallow at Mesa Verde* (Middle Creek Publishing and Audio, 2025). Used by permission.

"McGrath" from *North Dakota Quarterly* 83, no. 4 (Fall 2016). Used by permission of the author.

"Spiral Path" from *Stone Poetry Quarterly* (August 2023). Used by permission of the author.

DAVID MASON

"Another Thing," "Bristlecone Pine," "Fathers and Sons," "Hangman," "Kéfi," "Song of the Powers," and "The Soul Fox" from *The Sound: New and Selected Poems* by David Mason (Red Hen Press, 2018). Used by permission.

"Cold Fire" from *The Hudson Review* 76, no. 2 (Summer 2024). © 2024 by David Mason. Reprinted by permission.

"Cuttings" from *Arena Quarterly* 16 (Summer 2023). Used by permission.

"On the Shelf" from *Pacific Light* by David Mason (Red Hen Press, 2022). Used by permission.

"Stonewall Gap" from *Ludlow*, 2nd ed. (Red Hen Press, 2010). Used by permission.

MARY CROW

"Beyond Tahrir" published in *Hotel Amerika* 16 (Spring 2018). Used by permission of the author.

"Blind Spots" published in *Poet Lore* (Fall–Winter 2013). Used by permission of the author.

"Each Gets So Shamefully Little" published in *A Public Space* no. 10. Used by permission of the author.

"Eclipsed Horizon" published as "Intensity" in *The Vermont Literary Review*. Used by permission of the author.

"Everything in the Dream Is You" published in *Notre Dame Review*. Used by permission of the author.

"Fact Checking the Body" published in *Michigan Quarterly Review*. Used by permission of the author.

"Fault-Finding" from *I Have Tasted the Apple* by Mary Crow (© 1996 by Mary Crow). Reprinted with the permission of The Permissions Company, LLC on behalf of BOA Editions Ltd., boaeditions.org.

"Foreign Streets" published in *American Poetry Review*, reprinted in the collection *Borders*. Used by permission of the author.

"Getting Ready to Leave for Spanish Class, Granada, Nicaragua" published in *Apple Valley Review*. Used by permission of the author.

"The Missing Pages" published in *Sugar House Review*. Used by permission of the author.

"Scars" and "Travel" from *Addicted to the Horizon* by Mary Crow (© 2012 WordTech Communications LLC, Cincinnati, Ohio). Used by permission.

"What Was That City" published in *Adelaide Literary Review*. Used by permission of the author.

THOMAS HORNSBY FERRIL

"Always Begin Where You Are," "Beyond What Ranges?," "Here Is a Land Where Life Is Written in Water," "Magenta," "Nocturne at Noon—1605," "Noon," and "Noted" originally appeared in *Thomas Hornsby Ferril and the American West* by Thomas Hornsby Ferril (Fulcrum Publishing, 1996). Used by permission.

MILFORD E. SHIELDS

"Coyote," "Flowering Cloud," "San Juan Basin," and "These Things Are Free" from *Colorado and Other Poems* by Milford E. Shields (Bruce Humphries, 1943). Used by permission.

MARGARET CLYDE ROBERTSON

"Gold Rush," "Len B., Timekeeper," "Talk o' the Town," "Timberline," and "Tin Cup" from *Fool's Gold* by Clyde Robertson (Banner Press, Emory University, 1934).

NELLIE BURGET MILLER

"An Astronomer Muses" and "Masks" from *Pictures from the Plains and Other Poems* by Nellie Burget Miller (The Poets Press, 1936).

"I Have Loved Homely Things," "A Morning in an Old Library," "A Pagan in Church," and "Question" from *In Earthen Bowls* by Nellie Burget Miller (Appleton and Company, 1924).

ALICE POLK HILL

"Christmas Hymn," "I Am Not Ready," and "To Alice—My Namesake" from *Evenings with Colorado Poets*, edited by Frances Kinder and F. Clarence Spencer (Chain & Hardy Company, 1894).

ABOUT THE EDITORS

THIS ANTHOLOGY was edited by a committee of five Colorado poets laureate: Andrea Gibson, Bobby LeFebre, Joseph Hutchison, David Mason, and Mary Crow, supported by Turner Wyatt and Julia Seldin. The editorial committee gladly read through over a century of Colorado poetry to make these selections.

TURNER WYATT is the compiler of this book and the founder of the organization your purchase of it supports. The Colorado Poets Laureate Anthology is a nonprofit focused on increasing access to poetry in Colorado. Previously, he cofounded four award-winning social enterprises, including Denver Food Rescue, Fresh Food Connect, and Upcycled Food Association. Turner cofounded the Durango Poet Laureate Program in 2023 and served as producer for the award-winning documentary *Moving*

Line. He is a recipient of the Waste360 40 Under 40 Award, Top 20 Emerging Leaders in Food and Agriculture Award, and Young Leaders Award from Walking Softer and was a Fink Fellow. In 2015 he was appointed by Denver's mayor to serve on the Denver Sustainable Food Policy Council. Based in Durango, Colorado, Turner works as a writer, filmmaker, and social entrepreneur focused on projects that build more just and sustainable communities.

JULIA SELDIN is a nonprofit leader by day and a lover of poetry by night (and also by day). She has previously worked on two other poetry anthologies: *Courage: Daring Poems for Gutsy Girls* (Write Bloody Publishing, 2014) and *We Will Be Shelter: Poems for Survival* (Write Bloody Publishing, 2014). She is deeply honored to be part of the *Begin Where You Are* team and is thrilled to be continuing her work as a sidekick to poets in Colorado and across the country.